GET
STARTED IN
SELF-PUBLISHING

Kevin McCann and Tom Green

Teach Yourself®

Get Started in Self-Publishing

Kevin McCann and
Tom Green

First published in Great Britain in 2013 by Hodder & Stoughton. An Hachette UK company.

First published in US in 2013 by The McGraw-Hill Companies, Inc.

British Library Cataloguing in Publication Data: a catalogue record for this title is available from the British Library.

Library of Congress Catalog Card Number: on file.

10 9 8 7 6 5 4 3 2 1

Typeset by Cenveo® Publisher Services.

Printed and bound in Great Britain by CPI Group (UK) Ltd, Croydon CR0 4YY.

Hodder & Stoughton policy is to use papers that are natural, renewable and recyclable products and made from wood grown in sustainable forests. The logging and manufacturing processes are expected to conform to the environmental regulations of the country of origin.

Hodder & Stoughton Ltd

338 Euston Road

London NW1 3BH

www.hodder.co.uk

Also available in ebook

'Have something to say, and say it as clearly
as you can. That is the secret.'
Matthew Arnold

Acknowledgements

The authors would like to thank the following people: Nina Allen, Harriet Bourton, Martin Cloake, Jonathan Dean (Radio City, Liverpool), Vicci McCann (Senior Archivist, Lancashire Archives), Jimmy McGovern, Danielle McGregor (BSc. Hons, MSc.), Olivier Nilsson-Julien, Chas Parry-Jones (Ucheldre Literary Society, Holyhead), Victoria Roddam and Mel Sherrat.

Contents

About the authors

Kevin McCann *(www.kevinmccann.co.uk) is a professional writer with over 30 years' experience working in schools, libraries, hospitals, universities, community centres, care homes and prisons. He has published seven poetry collections for adults and his children's poems have been included in numerous anthologies. In 2011 he self-published a collection of ghost stories.*

He has contributed articles on the value of creativity to numerous magazines aimed at educationalists. In 2006 he was awarded the Booktrust's Writing Together Award in recognition for the work he has done in schools.

Tom Green *is a writer, playwright and scriptwriter. He edits the Writers' Guild magazine,* UK Writer *and the website www.writersguild.org.uk. His dramas have been performed on BBC Radio 4 and his stage play* Being Tommy Cooper *toured the UK in 2013.*

Introduction: Self-publishing – a revolution

One of the definitions of the word 'revolution' is *fundamental change* and that's what self-publishing is. Until comparatively recently it was an expensive process that was seen by many as an admission of failure. Self-published books were second rate and so, by implication, were their authors.

Not any more. Self-publishing, like guerilla film-making, is rightly recognized as being just as valid as the more traditional kind. As Oscar Wilde pointed out, the thing about any book is that it's either well written or badly written and that's all.

Of course, you'll still have to market the book yourself. On the other hand, you'll have a published book to market. It puts the final decision back into your hands.

There are detractors. Dire warnings of 'diluted quality', 'bursting bubbles' and something described as 'the inevitable backlash'. We think what lies behind this nonsense is the notion that writing – like all real culture – is the domain of the privileged few and that the rest of us should know our place and be grateful for our ghost-written biographies and oceans of cook books.

Leave it to the experts, they seem be saying, for they know best.

On the other hand, it's significant that, at the time of writing, a major publishing house has just bought into a self-publishing company. So either the company saw it as an important investment for the future or it just did it on a whim. Which, do you think, is more likely?

There have been more than a few major success stories in self-publishing. John Locke and Amanda Hocking both sold a million copies on Kindle and both went on to sign publishing deals with major publishers. So, yes, it is possible to make money self-publishing. Artistic integrity is all very well but writers have bills to pay just like everyone else.

Of course, there's no guarantee that everyone who self-publishes is bound for glory but one thing has changed for ever. Whether or not your book gets published doesn't depend on readers' reports, the market, who you are and who you know – though, to be honest, that last one's largely a myth. Whether your book gets published at all depends on you.

What self-publishing has done is to give ordinary people – though we both believe that everyone has the potential to be extraordinary – real choice. It encourages people to think for themselves and to have confidence in themselves.

When you publish your book, you will have achieved something marvellous. Writing a book isn't easy. If it was, there would be no need for ghost-writers.

Hopefully, you'll make some money.

And another thing: you will be helping to foster cultural diversity because, just as an ecosystem needs diversity to thrive, so does a culture.

What we'll do is share our combined knowledge and experience to teach you the skills and self-confidence to:

- redraft, proofread, edit and prepare your manuscript
- find the self-publishing option, or options, that best suits both your needs and your budget
- pick a title, design a cover, fix a price
- market your book so as to maximize your sales potential.

The chapters in this book have a practical outlook, with key advice and exercises to help you put what you have learned into action. Throughout this book you will see the following icons:

 Key ideas to help you hone in on what really matters

 Snapshot exercises that encourage you to carry out simple tasks that will get you on the road

 Workshop exercises – longer exercises that ask you to do a bit more work (there aren't too many of these, you'll be pleased to know)

 Write exercises – self-explanatory

 Edit exercises to help you get into the invaluable practice of reviewing your own work

 Focus points to help you take away the main points from each chapter.

We'll also show you all the potential pitfalls and tell you how to avoid them.

We'll introduce you to other writers who have already successfully self-published.

We'll aim to give you everything you'll need to maximize your book's chances of success.

Welcome to the revolution!

1

Begin at the beginning...

Kevin McCann

I was about 14 or so when I announced that I wanted to be a writer when I finally grew up. I was told by my careers advisor in school that writing wasn't a proper job. That clinched it for me. And later, when I was a student and met professional writers for the first time, a lot of them told me it was 'better than working'. So, like a lot of people, I imagined a life of ease interrupted by the odd flash of white-hot inspiration.

I was wrong, of course. It's a full-time job. It's hard work. The money's often lousy to non-existent. But you keep going anyway because you have no choice. You're in love and logic doesn't come in to it. So let's...

Why self-publish?

Four possible reasons spring to mind straight away:

1 **You love writing and you'd like to make some money.**
2 **You know it can take years for a book to go from final acceptance to actual publication and don't want to wait that long.**
3 **You've already had some work published and a book will help raise your profile.**
4 **You've been writing for years and now would like a book to distribute among your family and friends.**

You may have already tried submitting to publishers and/or agents and been politely but firmly rejected. The rejection will probably be brief because publishers receive hundreds of submissions every week and simply don't have time to give detailed responses. But it will have been read. Publishers/agents are in the business of making money and are always on the lookout for the 'next big thing'.

Of the thousands of manuscripts submitted every year, only a small number are accepted. So being rejected doesn't necessarily mean your book is bad. It may simply be that there are other books that are better.

Of course there are mistakes – one publisher's reader famously rejected the first Harry Potter book with the words, 'I can't imagine any child wanting to read this!' – but there are no conspiracies, just human error.

What is self-publishing?

The obvious answer is, in this case, the right one. Self-publishing means taking your manuscript and publishing it yourself. You can choose either to publish it as hard copy – that is, an actual book – or digitally as an e-book. There are a number of self-publishing companies that will enable you to do both.

This last option is worth considering as it will provide your potential customers (readers) with the all-important element of choice. It's true that in the last few years there has been an explosion in e-publishing and the sales potential on e-readers is huge. But it's also true that some readers prefer what they call a 'real book'. Not everyone has a computer or an e-reader, so keep your options open.

Before print-on-demand came into being, self-publishing was an expensive and, more often than not, soul-destroying process. You had to find a printer, pay for your book to be typeset and agree a minimum print run.

For every Roddy Doyle – who originally self-published *The Commitments* in 1987 – there were countless others who paid out small fortunes and ended up with boxes of unsold books gathering dust under their beds.

Or, worse, you might be conned by a vanity publisher who would print a limited number of poorly produced books and make a lot of promises about distribution that were never kept.

Now, for little or no initial outlay, anyone can get a book published. It will be a proper professional job and whether it gets published in the first place depends on you and nobody else but you.

But please keep the following facts in mind:

- **You'll need a computer and access to the Internet and you'll need to be computer literate.**

  In plain English, if you're a bit of a technophobe, it might be a good idea to see if there are any basic IT courses running in your local area. Using a computer is like any other skill. If it's clearly explained, it can be easily understood; and if it's constantly practised, it becomes instinctive.

- **You'll have to oversee every stage of the process carefully from first read through to final publication.**

  Again, there's nothing to be afraid of. The old proverb about the journey of a thousand miles starting with the first step couldn't be more applicable. Think of this book as your basic itinerary with maps and the Internet as tourist information. So don't worry. Help will be there whenever you need it.

- **You'll have to promote it yourself.**

  You'll have to learn about marketing so we'll be looking at social networking, the importance of blogs and websites, limited-edition free downloads – the equivalent of a special offer – plus all the other more traditional forms of marketing.

- **You'll need to be patient.**

  There are no short cuts, no magic words, no secret formulae and no lucky charms. You must be prepared to work hard and take infinite pains. There's really no other way.

Three quick tasks

Task 1 Type 'self-publishing companies' into your search engine.

Read through the services the various companies offer and the costs involved. A lot provide a complete package – editing, proofreading, cover design – and the costs are comparatively modest.

But what do you do if even 'comparatively modest' is outside your price range?

Well, there are sites where you can self-publish for no initial outlay at all.

Task 2 Type 'free self-publishing' into your search engine.

Have a look at the sites that come up and see if it's possible to upgrade further down the line. For example, can you initially make the book available on the company website and pay for additional help with marketing and distribution later on?

If you're unsure, contact the company in question. If they're helpful and open, they're legit. If they're evasive, move on.

Task 3 Type 'self-publishing e-books' into your search engine .

Again, have a look at the various sites that offer e-publishing and see which ones offer the kind of service you're looking for. You'll notice that they all offer step-by-step instructions or tutorials to guide you through the whole process.

'But I don't know whether I'm smart enough to do all that...'
On the pages of this book are individual letters. Each letter represents a sound. The letters (sounds) combine to make new sounds (words). These words then combine to make sentences. Your mind recognizes each letter, combines the sounds each one represents, reads the words produced, reads the sentences they make and then makes sense of them. It does all of that almost instantly, so following step-by-step instructions on a website shouldn't be too difficult. Try reading them aloud. I find it helps.

Remember something else as well: this whole process, from beginning to end, will involve you working in partnership both with this book and with the self-publishing company of your choice. How much or how little you spend will depend on your available funds. Of course, it would be easier to be able to afford one of the self-publishing companies that provide the full service. But if you're on a limited income it's still possible to do it all yourself and there are a couple of advantages to that:

1 **The smaller the initial outlay, the sooner you go into profit (providing the book sells).**

2 **You will gain new skills that will in turn add to your self-confidence. That's crucial. If you don't believe in yourself, why should anyone else?**

'I just want to make some money.' There's nothing wrong with that but it's not a case of either you make money or you write well. Shakespeare, Dickens and Kipling all wrote for money. The notion that the true artist is above such shabby commercial things is a myth. Nobody expects a doctor or teacher to work for free, so why should a writer?

Of course, we could argue for ever about what the difference is between a good and a bad book. Maybe a good working definition would be: 'A good book is one the reader wants to carry on reading.'

So it doesn't matter whether it's a romantic novel, a collection of poems, a biography or whatever... it should be the best it can be. If it's a good book, it should get good reviews, people will recommend it to other readers and your sales will go up.

Feedback

Every writer needs feedback. Those who claim they don't are either perfect (unlikely) or reluctant to admit it (deeply insecure). For the rest of us, though, honest feedback is crucial.

Why? Because you're simply too close to your own work. You've devoted a lot of time – years possibly – to writing a book and you may have become so devoted to it that you're blind to its faults.

It's understandable but it's also foolish. Nobody gets anything right 100 per cent of the time.

What's good? / What's bad?

Think of two films you've seen recently – one good and one bad. Then consider these three questions:

1 *What made the good film good?*

I'd guess it had a good script, was well acted and involving, and you kept watching to the end because you cared about the characters.

2 *What made the bad film bad?*

It probably had a bad script, was poorly acted, uninvolving and you cared so little about the characters that you stopped watching long before the end.

3 *Do you think anyone deliberately sets out to make a bad film?*

Well, of course not. Why would they? And think about all the films you've seen that began so well and then fizzled out. Is it just possible that what the director needed was someone to whisper in his or her ear: 'This just isn't working!'?

No matter how good the cover is, no matter how beautifully the contents are laid out, no matter how concise and punchy the blurb, if a book is badly written, nobody will want to buy it or read it.

So there are two things you need to find out:

1 Where can you go to get honest feedback?

2 How do you deal with negative criticism?

Family and friends will, I hope, read your work and be pleased for you. After all, writing a book is an achievement in itself. But they will be prejudiced. Their natural instinct – again, I hope – will be to be as supportive and therefore positive as possible. They'll tell you you're talented and brilliant and that your book is fantastic. All of which is very nice but, to be honest, next to useless.

What you really need is detailed unprejudiced criticism and there are a number of options available for this. If you're lucky enough to know a professional writer who's willing to look at your work and offer advice, follow that route. Otherwise you might like to consider one of the following.

WRITERS' WORKSHOPS

Ideally, what you're looking for is a tutor-led workshop. The tutor should be published and offer a course that includes regular criticism of your work, though don't be put off by this. It sounds negative but in a workshop it simply means advice.

So, with criticism, every negative should be counterbalanced with a practical positive. For example, if you're told that your short story was predictable, you should also be told how to fix it. If that's not the case, move on.

Workshops to avoid...

Avoid workshops that are really nothing more than mutual admiration societies. You'll learn nothing.

Find a writing course

Type 'writers' workshops' followed by your location into your search engine.

When the results come up, read each course description carefully. Some will be for absolute beginners, some will specialize in one type of writing – poetry, for example – and some will be aimed at the more experienced writer. And they will all cost money, so you need to decide whether, at this stage, you're both willing and able to spend some cash. If you can, find a course you can afford that suits your needs.

If you can't afford to pay at this stage, don't dismiss the idea out of hand. The chances are very high that somewhere close to home there is a writers' group that meets in a local school, college or library. Keep looking until you find one and sign up because, as every writer knows, some feedback is always better than no feedback at all.

WRITING MENTORS

Mentor: Experienced and trusted advisor (*Oxford Handy Dictionary*)

If you've already attended workshops and honestly feel you've gained all you can, you might want to consider getting yourself a mentor.

Some genre groups, like the Romantic Novelists (UK), do offer a limited number of places on mentoring schemes and, if you're a member of a writers' workshop, your tutor may offer a mentoring service. However, don't assume that they do. If they say no, leave it.

Find a mentor

Type 'online writing mentors' into your search engine. Read through the results and bookmark any that look interesting. Note not only the cost but exactly what you get for your money. What you want is both a detailed assessment of your work and specific advice as to how you can improve it.

WRITERS' GROUPS

These can be very useful particularly if you're a genre writer that is, you specialize in a particular type of writing such as crime, fantasy or romance. There are online chat rooms where you may find out about publishing opportunities/writing competitions as well as meeting other writers.

A lot of specialist genre groups have their own in-house publications. Some organize social gatherings, which can be great networking opportunities.

Attending a networking event

Before you attend a networking event have some cards printed with your name and contact details. Take them with you and be ready to give them to anyone who asks. Not only is it easier than scrabbling round with bits of paper and a pen, it makes a far better impression. And make no mistake, networking is important. We'll discuss why in a lot more detail when we get on to marketing proper. Facebook and Twitter are all very well, but there's no substitute for personal contact. Only give your cards to people who ask for them. Don't force them on anyone and never take copies of your book to networking events to sell. It creates a lasting bad impression.

Dealing with negative criticism

How should you deal with negative criticism? The wrong way is to get angry and simply dismiss it out of hand. The right way is to think about it. Good criticism is mainly concerned not with what your book says but how it says it.

For example:

- **Your work is underwritten.**

  Your book, at the moment, lacks readability. It doesn't hold the reader's interest.

- **Your story is difficult to follow.**

  This is a very common fault which springs from the assumption that because *you* know what's going on, so will your reader. What you need to remember is that you won't be there to answer questions or clarify any aspects of your book they find confusing.

- **It's full of clichés.**

  This one often provokes a strong reaction. The usual defence is that we all use clichés all the time. And of course that's true, but in conversation we're aiming to get information across; in writing, we're attempting to tell a story in a way that's both original and emotionally involving. The use of clichés works against this.

Now it may look as though these three examples are each about different problems. Well, on the surface they are. But once you go below the surface, they're really all about the same thing: the writer's use of language.

In other words, they're technical problems, which means:

- they're solvable
- solving them will immediately improve any book.

One last point: the criticism that annoys us the most is the criticism that we know to be true. It's rarely, if ever, what most of us want to hear. We'd all much rather be told, 'Don't change a word – it's perfect.'

Take criticism seriously

Faults in a manuscript need attention and, if you're serious about writing, you'll give it that attention.

Improving your skills

Writers' groups and mentors can take you only so far. What you also need to do is begin sharpening up your own critical faculty. This is the ability to tell the difference between good and bad writing in both yourself and others. And please don't worry that you won't be able to do that. You already can.

Think back for a minute. At the beginning of this chapter I asked you to think of two films you'd seen recently: one you thought was good and one you thought was bad. I then asked you to think about:

- the stories
- the dialogue
- whether or not you cared about the characters.

What you were actually doing was examining:

- plot structure
- use of language
- characterization.

You were using your critical faculty. It's been a part of you all your life and, if you haven't started already, it's time to begin developing it.

So how do you do that?

The importance of reading...

GENERAL READING

When children are learning to talk, they tend to copy the adults around them. Once they begin to develop their own individual personalities, so they develop their own way of expressing themselves. They may retain certain of their parents' mannerisms but they are not their parents. They have been influenced, not cloned.

The relationship between reading and writing works in much the same way.

If you read a lot of Raymond Chandler, you might begin writing bad Chandler pastiches. It won't last and you'll continue to evolve your own style. However, it won't have damaged you in any way. What you might gain is his ability to vividly describe a scene in three or four short snappy sentences.

So read widely and read whatever catches your eye.

Henry James, novelist

'A writer is someone upon whom nothing is lost.'

Brush up your reading

- What were the last three books you read?
- Of the three, how many were the type of books you have written / want to write?
- Are you a member of your local library? If not, then please join the very first chance you get. It's free and is a major writers' resource.
- Borrow a couple of books that were published no longer than five years ago.
- Read them (no need to make notes, just enjoy) and then go back and borrow more.
- When you find a writer whose work you really like, read as much as you can of that author.

MORE SPECIALIZED READING

You need to know as much as possible about the type of writing you want to do. If you don't already have one, get a copy of the appropriate Teach Yourself book. It will show you techniques to help you improve your writing immediately. It will also provide you with suggestions for further reading.

Of course, you may think you're beyond that stage. If that's the case, it would still be in your interests to at least look at the appropriate book.

What have you got to lose?

Start looking at books critically

Start looking at published books not just in terms of content but also titles, cover design, blurb and cost. Ask yourself: What is it about a particular cover or title that catches my eye? What makes me curious about a book that is written by an author whose work I don't know?

Is it the title, the cover design, the blurb or even the opening paragraph? Or is it a combination of all of these?

This is the beginning of market research, which Tom will be looking at in more detail in Chapter 2.

BACKGROUND READING

Biographies

If you're a novelist, as well as reading novels you might want to read some biographies. A good biography will not only give an account of a writer's outer life – the things they said and did – but of their inner life as well. For example, let's say you read a biography of a particular writer – someone whose work you really admire – and in it there's an extract from a letter in which they detail their working method or offer some advice on writing. Now think about that for a minute. A writer who may have been dead 20 years – as had Steinbeck when I first read *The Grapes of Wrath* – can still become, in effect, your teacher.

Critical books

Like biographies, critical books can be very useful but it really depends on your immediate needs and how deep you want to go at this stage. A good critical book should illuminate and increase your understanding. A bad one will almost always confuse.

Use your own good judgement.

Time out!

Of course, you could choose to ignore everything I've just said and go ahead and self-publish your book exactly as you wrote it because you're a genius. You know this to be true because your life partner / significant other / best pal told you so.

It's true that there are writers who have worked in total isolation and produced something utterly magnificent. You might even be one of them... but just to be on the safe side, why not get your work looked at, do some background reading and, for the moment, err on the side of caution?

Just in case you're wrong.

> ## Key idea: If a job's worth doing...
>
> The expression 'If a job's worth doing, it's worth doing well!' is a truism.
>
> It's a truism because it's true.

Back to your book...

By this point, hopefully, your work will have been read and commented on by other writers. They may have been members of a writers' group, a tutor and/or a mentor or a combination of all three.

Hopefully the criticism has been honest though not always what you've wanted to hear. But every negative should have been counterbalanced by a positive. So, bearing all that in mind...

Review your book

- Set the line spacing for your manuscript at one point five.
- Make sure the pages are numbered, and in the header/footer area put in your book's title, your name and the copyright symbol ©. Get into the habit of doing this with everything you write so it becomes automatic, like checking the rear-view mirror before you pull out into traffic.
- Print a copy.
- Read it. Don't worry about typos at this stage but, if you spot any, you might as well note them in the spaces between the lines.

- Ask yourself a very hard question: if this was by someone else, what would you honestly think?
- Write a short review, say 500 words or so. Remember, that for every negative there must be a positive.
- Summarize your review in two sections. In section one, briefly list your book's faults. In section two, list its strengths.

For example:

Faults:

- Story is confusing in places
- Some overlong descriptions

Strengths:

- Good ending
- Sharp dialogue

If you haven't already, go back and look again at the feedback you've already been given. Does any of it coincide with your own real feelings about your book? The chances are, some of it will, some of it won't. So, what should you do now? Well, for the moment, leave it. Put it away and go and do something else. Go out, catch up with friends and relax. You need to put some distance between you and your manuscript.

Think of it like this: next time you look at your manuscript, you'll do so with fresh eyes and a rested mind... which is exactly what you need.

In films, artists are often shown working themselves into a state of heroic exhaustion. They will then have some powerful vision and go on to produce a work of stark genius. The reality is that exhaustion leads to error. If you're driving and start getting sleepy at the wheel, you take a break.

Now, if you feel compelled to go on and begin redrafting, by all means do so. But, again, you need to be honest with yourself. If you just want to get the redrafting out of the way or you're trying to impress someone, or simply prove something to yourself, then take a break.

You don't just want your book to be good. You want it to be the best it can be.

Every book has a story

If your book is in the non-fiction genre, the above comments will still apply to what a lot of critics call a book's narrative. So, if it's a history, it's the story of a list of linked and significant events. If it's philosophy, it's the story of an idea or ideas. But the most important thing is: it needs to be as well written as you can manage to make it.

Focus points

- Find the self-publishing package that suits you.
- Minimal costs will maximize your profits once the book is published.
- Feedback can be illuminating.
- Negative feedback can be used as a roadmap for success.
- Your book needs to be well written.
- Your book needs to be well marketed.
- The last two points are of equal importance.
- Writers should also be readers, so read as much as you can.
- See reading not just as study but also as market research.
- Take your time. Hurrying any task leads to avoidable error.

Where to next?

In Chapter 2 we will introduce the subject of research and explore how important it is to the success of your project.

2

Research

Tom Green

Whether you are writing fact or fiction it is likely that research will be an important part of writing your book. Research might mean finding out specific things that will go directly into your book – for a local history, for example. Or it might be reading around a subject to increase your general understanding and help you shape your content.

Research matters because no one wants to publish work that gets things wrong. If people detect even small errors, it will damage your credibility as an author. If you want to be convincing, then you need to gain as much knowledge about your subject matter as possible.

In addition, it is important that you research the market for self-published books and the various services on offer.

Evaluate your research

Note down the key subject areas about which you are going to write and rate your knowledge about each one out of 10. Don't just choose the most obvious areas, include related ones as well. For example, if a character visits a psychotherapist, how much do you know about the treatment they will receive? Or, if you are writing a historical novel, consider all the aspects of people and places that you will need to know about. Be honest with yourself and where your mark is less than an 8 you probably need to do more research.

How to research content for your book

The Internet has made research much easier than it has ever been before. Huge amounts of information, opinion and analysis are available online, along with access to a large percentage of all the books that have ever been published. The key to successful research is focus.

When you first have an idea for a book your reading is likely to be at its widest. This is exciting, but it might also be daunting. On most subjects there are thousands of good sources of information and it can be hard to know how to navigate through them. It can be helpful to set yourself some time limits. Depending on how much research you think your book requires (some factual books or historical fiction might require substantial amounts), allow a certain number of weeks when you will be reading and researching.

Make sure you allow some time for general reading around the subject rather than just fact-hunting – even if you have a clear idea about your book, there's always the possibility of finding new insights that can change and develop your ideas. Once you have identified the key sources for research, set a time limit for each one. These limits should not be set in stone but they will guide you so that you do not lose yourself in one particular area and neglect another.

So, let's look in more detail at the various research resources that you can use.

Research matters

Research is an important part of the writing process for most books. Errors and inaccuracies will harm your credibility as an author. The aim should be to master your subject matter.

Research resources

THE INTERNET

It would be easy to spend many weeks researching almost any subject you can think of online. The depth and scope of information available is mind-boggling, so you will need a strategy to cope.

Search engines

For an overview of a subject, search engines such as Google or Bing will instantly list some of the most relevant and best-known sources. The results they produce are listed according to a range of factors, including relevance to your search terms and how many other sites link to them. They are not faultless, but as a starting point they are hard to beat.

Of course, what you find will depend on what you search for. These days search engines can often handle longer search terms quite well, so don't restrict your search and make sure you try different phrases. For example, if you are writing a book set in seventeenth-century France you could search on all of the aspects you feel you need to know about. So, you might start by searching on 'life in seventeenth-century France' and then move into more specific searches like 'food in seventeenth-century France', and so on. There will probably be some overlap in the results, but you will also discover new ones.

As you find relevant sites you will also want to follow links from them to other sources. As you click it's easy to get lost, so when you find a useful site make sure that you bookmark it with a note about what it contains.

All Internet browsers have bookmarks (also known as favourites) and it might be worth spending some time looking up how you can organize them – an Internet search on the browser name and 'managing bookmarks' will show you the way. Or you could simply copy and paste links as you find them into a document with a brief description.

Another option is to buy a project management tool such as Scrivener which has been designed to help authors manage data as they conduct research. It might take a little time to get used to, but it will help you organize your work and make it easy to rearrange and cross-reference information.

If you want to get really serious about research, you should look at the additional information search engines offer. For Google, go to www.google.com/insidesearch for advice, tips and tricks and discussion about doing searches. For Bing, visit the help section.

Video, audio and images

In most cases, search engines now include video and pictures as well as text on the main search results. However, if you want to search this content in detail, then you should visit the specific category that you want. For video, YouTube (owned and operated by Google) is by far the largest archive, and the search function works well. For sound files you might need to search a specific song or artist. You can also use Google music search www.googlemusicsearch.com. Images are probably the hardest thing to search for accurately, since the search engines rely largely on people labelling them accurately when they go online.

Wikipedia

If you search the Internet for almost anything, the Wikipedia page is likely to be one of the first results to be shown. Although, like any information on the Internet (or anywhere), it cannot be relied upon 100 per cent, for a general overview of a huge range of subjects it is hard to beat. Wikipedia pages also contain lots of links, so it is possible to read around a subject very quickly. The pages are maintained by volunteers, and it is open to abuse, but they have clear procedures to ensure as much accuracy in their information as possible.

Specialist websites

Many subjects will have specialist websites maintained by institutions or experts. These should have the benefit of being trustworthy and fairly comprehensive. They might also be able to put you in touch with people if you have specific research enquiries.

Discussion forums

Search engines often return results from discussion forums (also known as bulletin boards) quite high up their rankings and they can be excellent sources of information. There are discussion boards online for many different subjects and they are normally easy to search.

Most will have resident experts, not necessarily professionals whose opinion can be completely relied on but certainly people it is worth entering into dialogue with. And that, of course, is the benefit of discussion forums – you can register and then ask questions. As well as specialist forums, there are also general forums such as http://uk.answers.yahoo.com where you can submit any question.

Social media

Results from social media such as Facebook and Twitter won't normally show up on search engines to any great extent, but both of these sites are great places to ask questions. If you have lots of followers, you might get help directly. Or you could contact a relevant specialist person or agency via the social network and ask if they could put the question to their own followers for you. As with forums, the great benefit is that you will be able to have a dialogue with anyone who replies.

Try this

Ask a simple research question on Twitter or Facebook. If you don't get much response, search out some specialist people or agencies on Twitter and ask them directly.

Books

Despite the huge wealth of information on web pages, books and e-books remain a great resource for research. Bookselling sites, such as Amazon, can help right from the start – their search engines tend to be very effective and simply searching on a subject will often return numerous helpful results. Some books can be browsed online, others bought. The online market for second-hand books is now vast, with Amazon and Google Books providing the greatest range. Many e-books can be downloaded cheaply or even for free, including from the specialist free e-book site Project Gutenberg.

As increasing numbers of out-of-print books are made available on these sites, it is becoming rare for a book to exist that you can't trace online in some form. The only limits on your research are the cost of the book if it is still in copyright and the sheer scale of the task in finding the best books to read.

While you might start by browsing books, if there are too many for you to read it can be helpful to use forums on sites like Amazon, or social media, to ask for recommendations about the best books to read on the subject you are researching. Look also for books cited as sources in Wikipedia articles.

LIBRARIES

In pre-Internet days, research for writers was most likely to take place in libraries and they can still have a role to play. In the UK funding cuts have reduced library services in many areas, but they should still be able to order books you need and can often provide helpful advice and access to the Internet if you don't have that elsewhere.

Local libraries can be particularly useful for local history, since they will often have newspaper and other archives not easily accessible elsewhere. Local and regional newspapers are a fantastic first-hand source and are well worth seeking out both for specific research queries and to get useful background about a time and place. National newspaper archives are also useful

For specialist research the legal deposit libraries can be crucial. Legal deposit is the requirement for publishers and distributors in the UK and Ireland to place all published material in the six legal deposit libraries:

- British Library (London)
- Bodleian Libraries of the University of Oxford
- Cambridge University Library
- National Library of Scotland
- Library of Trinity College, Dublin
- National Library of Wales.

Each of these libraries has different regulations covering access, so you should check the website of any that you wish to visit. You will probably also need to do some planning before you visit and have a clear idea of the material you are seeking. You may need to order books in advance.

ARCHIVES

Most organizations, universities, government departments and agencies, museums and large companies will have archives of some kind. Access can be difficult, but if you are researching a specific subject then it is well worth trying to find archives relating to it. Some archives can be contacted online, although they normally charge a small fee for copying material. Others might not normally be open to the public, but if you can find the right person to contact, and can explain your interest, they might agree to let you see their materials.

The National Archive in Kew is the government's archive, holding information going back a thousand years. It has a huge amount of information online (including census records) at www.nationalarchives.gov.uk or you can visit them in person. However, if you are planning to visit, check the website first to see what preparation you need to do in advance.

The British Library runs the national newspaper archive (www.britishnewspaperarchive.co.uk). Work is ongoing to scan millions of pages of newspapers and the archive can be searched for free. A charge is made to download articles.

For access to the full British Library newspaper archive, you can visit the reading room in Colindale. Check the British Library site for registration details before you visit.

FILM ARCHIVES

A list of UK film archives can be found at http://filmarchives.org.uk. Film material can be difficult to access and you may be required to pay: for example, the British Film Institute (bfi) archive is available to the public by appointment and with a fee of around £10–15 per hour of running time.

INTERNATIONAL RESEARCH

The Internet can give you access to research materials around the world. Most public archives should be accessible, though you may have to pay a fee, and you should be able to find contacts in organizations or on social media sites and forums who can give you advice or answer specific queries.

For a list of online newspaper archives around the world, both free and paid-for, visit http://en.wikipedia.org/wiki/Wikipedia:List_of_online_newspaper_archives.

Make a list of possible resources

List how many different research resources you have used and consider which others might also be useful. Even if you're not sure what you're looking for, try something new. For example, do some searches on the British Newspaper Archive and the BFI National Archive and see what comes up.

Research across the board

The Internet is an incredibly powerful tool for resources but you can get overwhelmed. As well as browsing, seek out contacts in relevant organizations, libraries and archives who can help you. If possible, find people on Twitter and public forums who can advise you on where to focus your research.

Successful research methods

Whatever you are aiming to research, as a general rule it is best to start with a broad approach and then narrow down as you focus in on the most important elements for your book.

Even if you feel fairly confident about a subject, it's good to keep an open mind at the start and seek a wide variety of sources. There might be perspectives you hadn't considered before or information that causes you to rethink some of your views. Reading around the subject might also open up new areas for your work.

If you are new to a subject, the initial research is often a mix of the exhilaration of submerging yourself in new information and the frustration of having to plough through a huge amount that isn't relevant.

KEY SOURCES

Try to find out as early as possible in your research process what the key sources are on a given topic. Sometimes you can spend ages finding bits and pieces about a subject in various sources before discovering a single text that contains all the information and could have saved you weeks of work.

Ask around online or email relevant experts to get an idea about which websites, books or other sources people think are the most important. You might not want to restrict yourself to these, but they are a good place to start.

It's important to keep good records of your research as you go. Everyone will have different methods. Some people like to underline numerous passages in a book and make copious notes in the margin. Others prefer just the occasional reference to remind themselves where to find information at a later stage. Either way, while you don't want to lose yourself in writing notes that are too extensive, you will rarely regret taking a few moments to write something down, even if you are not completely sure of the relevance at the time. As mentioned above, you can use word-processing tools like Scrivener that have been designed to help authors manage projects from research through to a finished manuscript.

E-books provide new tools for keeping notes and references, and on Kindle, for example, you can also share your notes with others who download the book. As well as factual notes, it can be helpful to note down your own thoughts and ideas as they develop. For example, if you are writing a novel, you might have ideas about how the subject you are researching relates to one of your characters. The acts of researching your book and writing it don't need to be completely separate – use research to inspire ideas and note them down as they come.

After reading broadly to start with, you will probably need to narrow your research down into a particular aspect of a subject or a certain timeframe.

ACCURACY

At this point, when you are dealing with specific details, accuracy becomes important. You should never trust a single source, unless it is an original source – for example, you can't trust someone saying that a certain headline was used in *The Times* newspaper on a certain day, but you can find the headline yourself to verify it. Some secondary sources – that is, those that write from original sources – will seem more trustworthy than others. You might feel, for example, that you can trust the writing of an eminent historian but would need to verify something written by an unknown blogger.

Ultimately, the amount of time you put into verifying a fact or series of facts will depend on how important they are to your book and how much it matters if they prove to be incorrect. A minor detail in an historical novel that has no real bearing on the plot or characters might be tolerated, although it's still better to avoid them unless you are changing things deliberately. However, for anything that is central to your story or your argument, it's best to seek multiple sources and, where possible, go back to the original.

Remember this

Lots of websites use Wikipedia as a reference without citing it. If the Wikipedia entry is wrong, then lots of other sites might be wrong, too. So, if possible, check the references on a Wikipedia entry, to verify its accuracy.

DIFFERENT SOURCES

While you might prefer a certain research source, try not to restrict yourself to it. You are likely to be able to find different kinds of information in different kinds of sources, so try to vary your approach. It can be helpful to try a research source that you've never considered before. Even if your work has nothing to do with film, for example, a quick online search on a film archive might turn up results that you had never previously considered and open your mind to new avenues of research.

REFERENCES

If you want to get more deeply into a subject, follow up on references, links and bibliographies. In a print book these will normally be found at the end of a factual work, whereas links often occur throughout a piece online.

Be sceptical

Seeing something in print doesn't necessarily mean that it is true. Good researchers are always sceptical and look for the original sources of information so that they can judge its reliability.

Keep up to date

Are you familiar with the work of current experts in the fields about which you are writing? Whether it's fact or fiction, if you require research, you need to make sure that you have read what today's leading thinkers on the subject have to say.

When research stops and writing starts

Always remember that you are researching as a means to an end: to write a book. Hopefully, research will be an enjoyable part of the process but, if you are writing a book, it is not an end in itself.

So how do you know when to stop researching and start writing?

There are no easy answers. If you have a deadline for finishing your book – either external or self-imposed – then you will first need to decide how long you will need for writing and see how much time that leaves you for research.

It should be fairly obvious to you how important research will be and therefore how much time to allocate, but the research process is not always predictable. Sometimes it can take weeks to find the right information. On other occasions a source can throw up all kinds of new leads that demand to be followed up.

Ultimately, you, the author, must decide when and how to start your book.

Some writers keep the research and writing process quite separate. They will make notes as they go but, essentially, on a given day when they feel the time is right, they will put the books and Internet aside and begin to write.

For others, research and writing flow into each other. At any given point they might be furthering their research or writing, or both.

You must find the approach that suits you best.

The danger with separating research and writing is that you might not be aware of all that you need to research until you have started writing. Both factual and non-factual books can lead you in directions you don't expect and it would probably be foolish to rule out further research if you need it. You might also find it difficult to decide on the definite point where research ends.

However, if you carry on with research throughout the writing process, be wary of using it as a distraction. Most writers are good at finding anything to do other than writing and there might come a point when calling Internet browsing or half a day in the library 'research' is self-deluding.

Writing tends to be hard work, requiring intense periods of concentration. Some writers are able to switch between the writing and researching mindsets but, if you choose this approach, be aware that you might not be one of them!

Do a time-check

If you have written a book before, estimate how much time you spent researching and how much time writing. Was any of the research time wasted in self-distraction? Would you plan to spend more or less time on research for your next book?

DISPOSABLE RESEARCH

As a writer, one of the dangers of being an effective researcher is that you can find it hard not to use what you uncover. We're probably all familiar with reading novels where you can sense that the author has uncovered information they can't resist including – even when it runs to far greater length than the story requires. Some books are built on research, but be careful that you do not include information just because you have found it. Don't be afraid to leave things out. If something is fascinating but doesn't fit in the book you are working on, save it for the next one.

Copyright and plagiarism

It's important to respect copyright on any sources you use. In the UK 'Copyright is an automatic right and arises whenever an individual or company creates a work. To qualify, a work should be regarded as original, and exhibit a degree of labour, skill or judgement.' See http://www.copyrightservice.co.uk.

The duration of copyright varies depending on the form of the work, but for literary work it is 70 years from the end of the calendar year in which the last remaining author of the work dies.

Copyright law can get complicated and varies in different countries, but as a writer you don't want to risk legal action or getting a reputation as someone who breaches copyright: so err on the side of caution and always ask permission from the copyright holder if you want to quote from their work.

Copyright can be waived by the copyright holder and this sometimes happens through what are called Creative Commons Licences. See www.creativecommons.org.uk.

PLAGIARISM

Plagiarism – passing off someone else's work as your own – is a very serious issue for a writer.

Sometimes it is unintentional. For example, during your research you might note down a useful passage of text and forget to put an attribution with it. Then, weeks or months later when coming to write, you paste the text into your manuscript as if it were your own.

You might consider this a harmless mistake, but the original author will not. So you need to be very careful to ensure that work in your name is by you. Plagiarism is a kind of fraud and should be avoided at all costs.

For more information about plagiarism, see www.plagiarism.org.

 Remember this

Self-published work is covered by the same laws of copyright and libel as work published by corporations. Be aware of your legal and moral responsibilities as an author and, if in doubt, ask a professional for advice.

Market research

At each stage of the self-publishing process it is helpful to learn as much as you can about books you might be competing with or services you might buy. It's hard to write any book without an awareness of the market for that type of publication, and it might actually inform your work to a large degree – for example, if you can see the kind of works that have been successful or can identify gaps in the market.

Throughout this book we will also be recommending you research the market of fellow authors and service providers at every stage. For example, it is useful to see which cover designs work well, which formats suit which kind of book and how successful authors use social media.

Focus points

- Whether writing fiction or non-fiction, research matters. Inaccuracies will damage your credibility as an author.
- It's easy to get overwhelmed by the number of research resources available. If you have a publishing deadline in mind, make a timetable and restrict your research to a certain number of weeks or months.
- Start research by getting a good overview of a subject and then narrow down.
- Ask for help and advice from experts via email or on social networking sites and forums.
- Be aware of copyright laws and never plagiarize someone else's work.

Where to next?

In Chapter 3 we will look at how you can improve your manuscript and develop your visual imagination.

3

Redrafting

Kevin McCann

OK, so you've read your book, spotted some typos and written a 500-word review. At this point you may be experiencing one of two dangerous extremes. You could be thinking, 'It's brilliant – I need not change a word!' or 'It's dreadful – what a fool I've been!' Both are dangerous because both invite you to ignore your own intelligence. The chances are it's not ready either for publication – yet – or the bin.

What it will need now is work.

A plan of action

When redrafting, use the following plan of action:

1 Draw up a timetable/schedule and stick to it. Ideally, it should be a couple of hours per day but no less than three sessions per week.

2 In each of those sessions carefully proofread your manuscript.

3 At this stage you're looking for typos, punctuation errors and missing words – in other words, obvious mistakes.

4 Correct as you go along and aim for a minimum word count checked per session.

5 Take a ten-minute break every half-hour or so.

Keep a notebook and pen handy. As you're checking, ideas for additional material, plot or structure changes, for example, may occur to you. Note them down for future reference and then get back to the checking. If you stop and start rewriting at this stage, you'll never finish.

If you come across a section that's typo-free but somehow doesn't feel right, try reading it aloud. I find that problems with sentence construction that can't always be seen are glaringly obvious when heard.

Write a chapter-by-chapter summary as you go along. You may think you know your book inside out already. After all, you wrote it. The problem is that you're now so involved that making an objective assessment is probably impossible. Writing a summary will give you some distance as well as a complete overview.

When you've finished, read your summary, put it away for 24 hours (at least) and then read it again.

Pause for a story

Michelangelo was buying marble from a quarry just outside Rome. After he'd selected the pieces according to size, quality, etc., he noticed a chunk that was being used as a doorstop. It was green, uneven and looked good for nothing except being used as a doorstop. He asked the quarry owner how much he wanted for it. The owner was baffled.

'Why do you want that?' he asked.

Michelangelo smiled and then replied, 'Because when you look at that marble all you see are its flaws. But when I look at it, I know there's an angel trapped inside and, with my chisel, I'm going to set it free.'

By summarizing and reading (then rereading) your summary, you should begin to see both the strengths and weaknesses in your book's plot even more clearly. You should also have realized that a good original idea is, in itself, not enough. As a creative writing tutor I've sat and listened to dozens of great ideas for stories. Then I've listened to the stories themselves and watched the face of the writer as she/he begins to realize that it's just not working. And the main reason the story didn't work was because it didn't involve. And the reason it didn't involve was because it was badly written.

So what exactly do I mean by that?

For me, it means any piece of writing that lacks evidence of either craft or talent. Now, you can't teach talent. There are no 'seven steps to true genius', but you can maximize the talent you possess.

And how do you do that?

The same way Michelangelo, Shakespeare or any other artist has done – by hard work and practice. It's true that there are no short cuts but there are any number of techniques you can use that will immediately improve your work.

For example, is your book too wordy? Are you, like me and everyone else who writes, just head over heels in love with words? Are you using whole pages where a few sentences will do?

Pause for a bad joke

The last man in the world can't stand the loneliness any longer. He climbs up to the top of the Empire State Building and jumps. As he passes an open window on the twelfth floor, he hears a phone ringing.

I know it's not exactly a thigh slapper but it does illustrate a point. The joke begins with the last man in the world. We're not told how he ended up as the last man or where he lives. We work out it's the USA because of the Empire State reference.

Your opening pages

Take the first two pages of your book, copy and paste them into a new document and note the exact word count.

Next, have a look at your opening sentence. What you want is to grab your reader's attention and make them want to read on. An excellent example of this is the opening sentence of Graham Greene's thriller *Brighton Rock*.

> *Hale knew, before he had been in Brighton for three hours, that they meant to kill him.*

Who wants to kill him? Why? Why doesn't he either go to the police or leave town? The only way to find out is to read on.

Go back to your opening sentence. Does it make you want to read on? Is your real opening sentence further in? One thing I've noticed running writers' groups is how many people begin a story by setting the scene. They'll introduce details the reader (at that stage) simply doesn't need.

Finally, read your extract aloud and listen for the point where the narrative actually begins. You'll know it when you hear it. It'll be like that moment when a dull film suddenly, and unexpectedly, gets interesting. That's your *writers' instinct*. It's an ability we all possess; only most of us call it intuition.

The first rewrite...

The first rewrite is almost always about cutting words.

Notice I've said 'almost always' because there are no absolute rules in writing and redrafting. You want to cut everything you don't need but you don't want to end up with something that reads like notes. That's where judgment comes in.

Edit exercise

Go back to your extract and delete every word you don't need.

When you've finished, read it aloud. If it's awkward to say, it will be awkward to read. So:

- Are some of the sentences still just too long?
- Can you split them into shorter sentences?
- Can you delete some of them and still keep your meaning?
- Are they difficult to say because the word order is awkward?
- Does it read like a bad translation from another language?
- Does it contain more information than you need?

Go back through the extract again and, when you've finished, check your word count. You'll have lost words but the chances are you'll have gained greater clarity.

Ted Hughes, poet

'... *imagine what you are writing about. See it... When you do this, the words look after themselves like magic.*'

Think back to Michelangelo's angel. When he saw that lump of marble, he imagined the angel inside it. He visualized it. When you write, aim to do the same thing.

How? Again, let's think about films:

Q: How does a film tell a story?

A: By combining dialogue and action – words and pictures.

Q: How does a writer tell a story?

A: By combining dialogue and description – words and pictures again.

Anton Chekov, writer of short stories and plays

'*Cut out all those pages about moonlight... Show us the moon's reflection in a piece of broken glass.*'

Let's think about reading. In Chapter 1 I talked about what's actually involved in the process itself – recognizing individual letters and the sounds they represent, combining those letters into words, the words into sentences and so on.

What I want to talk about now is how words on a page interact with your imagination.

Think back to your own childhood. When you were reading, or being read to, what effect did the words have on your imagination? I'm not thinking here about the abstract – 'they fired my imagination' – but the concrete. In my case, then and now, the words on the page generated images in my imagination – my mind's eye, if you like. And the more precise, concise and exact the description, the more my imagination was stimulated.

This, in turn, affected my emotions, which engaged me even more. But if the description I was reading was vague or even confusing, then I'd have to stop and reread that section again and this created a barrier between my imagination and the words on the page.

So what you're looking for are *images:* word pictures that are immediate and vivid.

Show emotion

Think of an emotion. Now think of a character feeling that emotion. In no more than 50 words, show that character experiencing that emotion without naming it.

For example:

Mary leaned against the back wall staring out of the window. Rain fell steadily. Her students were all making notes and the room was silent. She glanced at the clock. Three-twenty. Still forty minutes to go before the lesson finally ended.

'My hands', she thought, 'look old.'

(Word count: 47)

The emotion I was attempting to invoke was depression and, apart from drawing on my own memories, I used a few cinematic devices. Think of the passage as a clip from a film.

Medium close-up: Mary leaning against classroom wall.

Cut to: View outside – rain.

Cut to: Panning shot of classroom then up to clock.

(Silence except for ticking clock.)

Voice-over: Forty minutes to go.

Close up: Mary's hands.

Voice-over: My hands look old.

 F. Scott Fitzgerald, novelist

'Action is character.'

Look again at the short passage about Mary, our depressed teacher. I could have written a much longer piece beginning:

> Mary stood at the back of her classroom and looked out of the window at the pouring rain. *The weather matched her mood.* She was depressed and the afternoon *dragged at a snail's pace.* Her students wrote silently and the clock's ticking *reminded her of the fact that time was passing...*

Now, apart from the fact that it's too wordy, it tells you what to feel (the weather matched her mood), it uses a cliché (snail's pace) and explains the symbolism of the ticking clock. The first version contains all the same information but in just 47 words. It also only takes about 20 seconds to read aloud, so halve that for silent reading. If the passage was twice as long, it would take twice as long to read. It would affect the pace of the story.

In a film, if the action and dialogue race along too quickly, it becomes difficult to follow and, therefore, uninvolving. If it goes too slowly, your attention wanders and you lose interest altogether. It's the same with writing. You have to vary the pace. Short sentences speed up the pace. Longer ones slow it down. So avoid:

- **Padding** This is needless detail. Try to give the reader an impression of each character but don't provide them with something that reads like a description issued by the police. In Alan Sillitoe's short story 'Uncle Ernest', we're told that Ernest makes his living as a furniture upholsterer, that he smokes and that his clothes are shabby. We're not given any more because we don't need any more. We can imagine the rest for ourselves.

- **Clichés** It's OK to use clichés in dialogue or if your main character is telling the story, but it's never acceptable to use them in descriptive passages. Either cut them altogether or replace them with better descriptive phrases.

- **Unnecessary dialogue** Dialogue requires purpose. In other words, it's no good just slotting in a few lines of dialogue every now and again to fill up another half page and get you that bit closer to writing THE END. It must all be adding to the story.

It's also important to remember that most people don't speak in perfectly formed sentences. Nor do they always get straight to the point.

If you're not sure about a section of dialogue, again, try reading it aloud. If you're having trouble following what your character is saying, what chance will your reader have?

It's equally important to remember that a story is not real life. It may be inspired by real people and events, but those real people, the things they say, and events must then be shaped into a coherent story.

Cut, cut, cut...

In your book, anything that's not needed, whether it's a page, a paragraph, a sentence, a phrase or even a single word, should be cut.

At this point you could be forgiven for thinking 'I can't do all that!' and, of course, you don't have to. You could sort out the typos, tidy it up a bit and then publish – and within six months be ashamed to have your name on the cover.

Or you could go on the Internet and cost the complete editing, design and publishing package. You could even get the whole thing ghost-written – that is, get a professional writer to rewrite your whole book for you, so that only your name appears on the cover (and you'll feel about as involved with 'your' book as a ghost feels involved with its former life).

However, there are two counter arguments:

1 You've already invested a lot of time and energy writing the first draft. Was that all for nothing?

2 Of course you can do it. You already know the difference between good and bad writing because you read. Simply put, a good (well-written) book makes you want to read on. A bad (badly written) book doesn't.

I know it looks daunting and I know I've given you a lot to think about. And I haven't mentioned the word 'inspiration' once. Don't worry, I'm getting to it.

Let's summarize the story so far:

- Check through your manuscript slowly and carefully. Do not skim or speed read. Note all the typos, missing words, punctuation errors, and so on. In other words, start with the obvious.
- Correct as you go along.
- Summarize your book, chapter by chapter, as you go along.
- If ideas for plot changes and so forth occur to you, note them but keep going.
- When you've finished, read your summary, then give yourself a few days off.
- Go back to your book and again, slowly and carefully, cut out verbiage, clichés and padding – like Michelangelo, chip away anything you obviously don't need. Once you've done this, your angel will begin to emerge.
- Your descriptions of people and places should be precise and visual – think film here – so that your reader 'sees' the story in their mind's eye.
- Evoke emotions – don't just name them. Don't tell me that someone's depressed, make me feel their depression – let me see the world through their eyes.
- Make sure your dialogue rings true and moves the story on.
- If in doubt, read it aloud. Or, better still, record your reading and then listen to it.

Now, as I said, you don't have to do any of that. However, I'd strongly advise that you to give it a try. The first and, to me, most obvious reason why you should is that writing is a skill and, like any skill, the more you practise, the better you become.

The second reason, not quite so obvious but equally valid, is that underachievement (the thing bad teachers call failure) is almost always linked to low self-esteem. Well, the reverse is also true. If you redraft slowly, carefully and systematically, and follow the suggestions I've made, your book will be improved – and it will be you who has improved it. By doing so, you will have sharpened up your writer's instinct, gained in confidence and, most of all, made an important discovery: redrafting is hard work, very tiring, seems to take for ever and can reduce you to tears. However, when it's going well, it's exhilarating, addictive, energizing and, ultimately, profoundly satisfying.

Readability

When you're redrafting, keep asking yourself the following question: What do I want my reader to get out of this?

Whether your book is fiction or non-fiction, it's still a narrative whose aim is to fully engage the reader's intellect and imagination. Notice here that I've said intellect *and* imagination. It's not a case of either one or the other. It should always be both. If your book is a thriller, you want your readers to feel thrills. If it's a comedy, you want your readers to laugh. If it's non-fiction, then you want your readers to come away with a clearer understanding of your subject matter.

What it should never be is an uninvolving insult to the reader's intelligence.

And just for the benefit of anyone thinking, 'Doesn't apply to me. My book's aimed at five-year-olds!' think again. Young children will accept fantasy and even apparent illogic, but they won't sit still long for a story that contains no internal logic. The logic may be crazy – at night, beds fly, toys come to life when nobody's looking, monsters have big teddy bears – but it must make some kind of sense.

So what makes you start reading a particular book? What makes you want to carry on? What makes you glad you did?

I suspect that most of us would give the same three answers:

1 The book's title/blurb/cover caught my attention.
2 The first page drew me in straight away and the rest of the book held my interest.
3 I gained something by reading it.

Depending on the book, what each reader gains will be different. I gain knowledge from non-fiction and I gain pleasure from fiction. Then again, I also read critical books for pleasure and I've read novels that have increased my knowledge. I often start a particular book because I'm either researching something or it's been recommended to me, or both. But there's only ever one reason why I finish a book: because I want to.

Why do I want to? Because it draws me in and holds my attention, and what holds my attention is a lot more than just good content. A well-researched but badly written book, whether it's fiction or non-fiction, will soon be discarded.

Interestingly enough, a correctly written book, one that's grammatically perfect, contains not a single typo, and so on, but is profoundly uninvolving, will often suffer the same fate.

The thing that they both have in common is contempt for me, the reader. The badly written book assumes that I'll read any old trash to pass the time. The correctly written book assumes that I'll be so impressed by someone who can spell, I won't notice how dull and lifeless the content is. But the well-written book, the one I always finish, assumes:

- I'm reasonably intelligent and can understand most things if they're explained clearly.
- I really don't like being told what to think.
- I can tell the difference between a fact and an opinion.
- I want to feel both imaginatively and emotionally engaged with any book I'm reading.

Inspiration

There is a myth that Van Gogh was a self-taught, blindly inspired genius whose greatest works were knocked out at the rate of five or six a week. The truth is that Van Gogh was a genius and that he was prolific in the last few years of his all-too-short life. What is also true is that he spent the preceding years practising and perfecting his skills. He would paint and repaint the same landscape until he got it absolutely right. In a letter to his brother, Theo, he uses the phrase 'Now my brush stroke is sure'. What he means is that constant practice has made his craft instinctive and that now he'll be able to fully realize his vision.

So am I saying that inspiration is a myth and that all art, whether it's painting, sculpture or, in our case, writing, is nothing more than the product of techniques that anyone can learn?

The short answer is no.

We're all born a blank page and our experiences shape us into the people we become. It's true that there are common factors in the early lives of writers – they include a solitary childhood, a rich fantasy life, a near-death experience... I know the full list by heart because when I was a teenager I read *The Poet's Calling* by Robin Skelton. In a chapter called 'The Child and The Muse' there was a long list of common factors in the early lives of poets. I eagerly read through it and found, to my joy, that I had the lot.

Excellent, I thought. Everything I write will be brilliant!

Five years and several hundred rejection slips later, I decided to have a rethink. I went back to Robin Skelton's book and read the chapters I'd originally skipped. The ones about craft and study. The ones I thought I didn't need to read. Why should I? I'd scored a perfect ten on the checklist so I was obviously beloved of the gods.

So, again, am I saying inspiration is a myth?

Well, again, no.

So, if it's not a myth, what is it?

In my experience inspiration is that point in any piece of writing when craft, imagination and emotion converge and, as Ted Hughes put it, the words take care of themselves. It's the intuitive leap that bypasses logic and amazes you, the writer, as much as it will amaze your readers. It won't grow out of software or templates any more than Van Gogh's best work could have grown out of painting-by-numbers.

You can believe that it's sent by God, the muse or your subconscious; it doesn't really matter. What does matter is that you recognize it when it arrives. And when it does arrive, you'll need to have developed the necessary level of skill to be able to take that imaginative raw material and transform it, make it as real and vivid for your readers as it is for you. So:

1 Carry a notebook and pen, or something to make notes on, at all times.

2 If a sentence, phrase, description, etc., comes into your head, even if it's not apparently related to your current project, note it down.

3 When you're working on your book, if a strong idea that will take your story in a new and unexpected direction won't leave your head, go with it!

CAN INSPIRATION BE INDUCED?

The short answer is no, but you can create conditions that will make you more receptive to it:

- Continue reading widely.
- As well as the appropriate Teach Yourself book, have a look at more books on writing.

One last thing. Like Van Gogh, you will gain from regular practice. You need to 'sketch' regularly. One very simple but incredibly useful exercise is the daily haiku.

> **Haiku:** three-line non-rhyming poem originally from Japan. It is usually 15 syllables – line one is five syllables, line two is seven and line three is five again. What it aims to do is capture a moment. For example:
>
> *Clearing the bar, she*
> *Falls through silence and into*
> *All that unleashed breath.*

The beauty of haikus is that they're economical (and therefore help you practise economy), mainly visual (so sharpen up your use of visual imagery) and, if you get into the habit of writing them regularly, they will become instinctive. This, in turn, will carry over into your other writing.

There are two things to bear in mind here. Firstly, the rules regarding syllable count are blurred. If the haiku is a translation, then the syllable count can vary; but if they are new and original, as yours will be, then in my opinion it is non-negotiable. Anyone who tells you differently is, again in my opinion, simply wrong. If you stick to the rules, you'll find that working within a strict discipline will make you more, not less, creative.

Secondly, don't expect instant results. The chances are that to begin with your haiku will be very 'So what?' Stay with it and cultivate patience – think tortoise and hare here – because there is still a long way to go.

I mentioned in Chapter 1 that writers should also be readers. I'll take it as a given that you've already looked at other Teach Yourself books directly related to your chosen field. Here are two more, one technical book and one e-bulletin, that I urge you to read:

- **The Art of Fiction** by **David Lodge**: In this the novelist and critic David Lodge looks at the opening pages of 50 different novels. He analyses and explains, in an accessible and readable style, a whole range of technical terms such as magic realism and in the process will introduce you to ways of telling a story you may never have heard of, let alone considered using. Each chapter is roughly four pages long and can be read in about ten to fifteen minutes. It is one of the best books of its kind I've ever read.

- grammar.guide@about.com: E-bulletin packed with useful articles on writing.

There are some more ideas for helpful reading at the end of this book.

Focus points

- Your first redraft will deal mainly with typos and other obvious errors.
- Make notes for possible plot changes and so on as you go along but don't start the rewrite yet.
- Your first redraft will be the first of many.
- Write a chapter-by-chapter summary as you go along.
- Initially, redrafting is almost always about cutting.
- Don't tell me what to see – make me see it.
- Don't tell me what to feel – make me feel it.
- Inspiration is not enough – you need skill as well.
- So write regularly *and*
- Read!

Where to next?

In Chapter 4 we will look at how to prepare your manuscript for publication.

4

Preparing your manuscript for publication

Kevin McCann

So far we've talked about the need for economy, accuracy and precision. By now you should have read through your manuscript, checking for typos, grammatical errors, clichés, padding and every individual word you don't need. You should also have written a chapter-by-chapter summary.

So, are you finished and ready to publish? Well, the chances are, no.

Victoria Roddam, publisher

'Self-publishing should be, in fact, more beholden to the rules of quality and form than traditionally published work, as it stands alone with no marketing, "community" or author personality smokescreen.'

There will be typos and other assorted mistakes in the text that you won't have spotted yet because you're too close and too involved in the book. You may even be wondering if you really want to carry on.

If that's the case, take a break. Catch up with some reading, go for some solitary walks, bake another cake and put some distance between yourself and your book.

Don't leave it too long before you get back to it, though. One month can give you the objectivity you need. Three could kill your momentum completely.

Readers' groups and...

At the time of writing, a lot of libraries still host readers' groups. They meet at regular intervals, usually once a month, to discuss a book they've all read. The books are loaned by the library hosting the event. Joining one will help your development as a writer by sharpening up your critical faculty – once a month you'll be discussing plot, structure and characterization with a group of readers, so it will also be market research. What better place to find out about people's reading habits than a readers' group? You'll be introduced to writers whose work you may not have considered previously. This will broaden your knowledge and monthly meetings will provide structure to your writing life – writing is self-discipline; self-discipline grows out of structured routine.

...self-education

Back in the 1960s there was a debate going on in educational circles which could be summed up as: 'Spelling and grammar: taught or caught?' On one side there were the advocates of free learning, with the traditionalists on the other. Most practising teachers were in the middle.

Free learning meant that children chose their own topics to study, corrected their own work and were self-motivated. The traditionalists favoured grammar, spelling tests, learning by rote and lots of testing. Obviously, there was a lot more to it than that. I'm oversimplifying for the sake of brevity.

Those in the middle realized that there's no one-size-fits-all way of learning. Some of us learn by listening, some by doing and some by a mixture of both. It wasn't taught or caught. It was both, and the best way to educate the individual child was the way that worked best for them.

What most teachers did agree on was that self-discipline grew out of structured routine. Traditionalists believed that an imposed structure (and the discipline that went with it) would always be required. Progressives believed that, once children became self-motivated (i.e. they could see the point of gaining knowledge), the imposed structure would fade and be replaced by self-motivation, which would in turn lead to greater achievement. What everyone did agree on was that the purpose of education is to help the individual child realize their full potential.

Education: From the Latin *educo* – to draw out.

That's your aim as well. You want to realize your full potential as a writer. You're both student and teacher. True, you've also got Tom and myself, the Internet, writers' groups, friends, family, a whole support network, in fact. But, in the end, it will always come back down to you, the words and how well you get on together. So you need to consciously and realistically recognize the gaps in your knowledge and address them by constant reading. As well as reading more, you should start to become more discriminating, and joining a readers' group will help you do just that.

The Irish novelist Edna O'Brien once said that if you read rubbish, you'll end up writing it. Of course you might respond with, 'And who decides what's rubbish?' The answer is, of course, that ultimately you will.

You already discriminate when it comes to films and TV shows – at least I hope you do. You begin by applying those same feelings to whatever it is you're reading.

It was, and still is, accepted by good teachers that underachievement is often the result of low self-esteem. Low self-esteem manifests itself either as 'Can't do this – I'm thick' or 'Not doing this – it's boring'. In adults this becomes a kind of militant anti-intellectualism. And, sadly, I've often come across it in would-be writers. They either put their faith entirely in inspiration or claim that reading other people will somehow dilute the purity of their vision.

It's like offering somebody a compass and detailed map showing the best route through the forest, only to find yourself glibly refused with the words, 'No thanks, I've decided to put all my faith in dumb luck.'

You may feel that you're a reasonably well-read, open-minded kind of person and that none of this really applies to you. You may even be right... but are you sure you're not just being complacent?

Go back and read the quote at the beginning of the chapter again. Victoria Roddam is not saying your book should be as good as something published by Bigname Publishers; she's saying it's got to be better than that.

So step one is to make sure that it's well crafted. You can, of course, use the spellchecker and then go back and proofread it again. A spellchecker will highlight 'teh' but won't tell you whether you typed 'pole' instead of 'pale'.

Don't use the auto-correct. This only leads to more errors as your computer (unlike you) is incapable of making informed decisions. I once used the auto-correct on an article I was writing and it altered the name of the self-publishing company FeedARead to Breastfeed.

Rely entirely on software and you'll learn nothing at all. If you're not prepared to learn, how can you ever expect to improve?

If you don't think your book is worth all that extra effort, you obviously don't really believe in it. If you don't believe in it, why should anyone else? Why should they part with money and give up their time to read something you think 'will do'?

You owe it to your potential readers, but you also owe it to yourself, not to fall into that trap. You might even tell yourself that that's the best you can do. You might even believe it. Well, for a while at least. But if you're developing your writer's instinct, you will carry on. As well as making sure that your book is free of all the obvious errors, you may begin to sense that it needs something else as well.

Harriet Bourton, fiction editor

'There must be an interesting, engaging and emotive voice coming through. If I can't hear that voice in my head when I read it, I know that, regardless of how well plotted it is, I just won't love it. And if I don't love it, I won't rave about it to my colleagues, who are essentially the people who'll eventually be the ones to sign off on whether we can buy it. What's difficult is that you can't force a voice in fiction – it's either there, or it's not.'

In his essay on Dickens, George Orwell said that he always got the impression that somehow Dickens was speaking directly to him. Incidentally, if you've never read any of Orwell's essays, do so. They're not only insightful but also models of clarity. 'Decline of the English Murder' is an excellent starting point.

The point that both Harriet Bourton and George Orwell are making is this: a well-crafted, well-plotted book is simply not enough. What makes any book, fiction or non-fiction, stand out is the writer's voice.

Think of it like this. Two people tell the same joke. They both use more or less the same words and both arrive at the same punch line. When A tells it, everyone falls about laughing. When B tells it, people smile politely but no one so much as giggles. Why?

Because A knows when to pause, what to emphasize and how to bring the joke to life. B, on the other hand, merely tells you what happened. One is a living story; the other is only a description.

So how do you find your voice?

Well, as Harriet Bourton rightly points out, you can't force it but you can develop it. So as well as reading widely in your chosen field, read book reviews, magazine articles and also have a look at writers' blogs. The best ones are always interesting. You could also consider starting one of your own. If you type 'starting a blog' into your search engine, you'll find various free sites as well as online tutorials showing you how to set one up.

Tom goes into blogging in more detail in Chapters 9 and 10 so you might want to jump ahead and read that section as soon as you feel ready. Just come back here once you're done.

Incidentally, you might think that, if you've written non-fiction, all of this 'writer's voice' stuff doesn't really apply to you. You're wrong. Remember: whether you've written fiction or non-fiction, you've still produced a narrative (story). It might be the story of a specific period of history and its significance or a sci-fi extravaganza, but if it doesn't hold the reader's attention from beginning to end, then it's a failure.

Think back a moment to when you were a child. When you were listening to a story (as opposed to reading it yourself) what was it that held your attention? The content, the storyteller's voice, or both? What made A a better joke teller than B?

You could be forgiven for thinking, 'He's given me all this to think about, I'm redrafting my book and now he suggests writing something else!' What I'm actually suggesting is that you begin working on smaller projects that will complement your book and bring you one step closer to finding your authentic voice.

Because you've got one and it's exactly the voice Harriet describes. You can't force it, but you can now take further steps to help release it.

Finding your voice

One very good way of doing that is writing a blog. In fact, get into the habit of writing whenever you can. Get a Facebook page, comment on whatever you like and do so regularly. Make it part of your daily routine. I log into Facebook once a day. I try to make it roughly the same time every day and I put a time limit on myself. It's not just that I don't want to spend half my life Facebooking; it's also because time limits, like deadlines, concentrate the mind.

And, again, you're speaking in your own voice.

You might want to consider article writing. I used to write for the novelist Helen Watts when she edited educational magazines aimed at literacy teachers. I usually had a couple of weeks to get each piece written and I always had a word count of 1,500. I found writing the first one really heavy-going. A full week had gone by and I only had about 400 words to show for it. 'What the hell's the matter with you?' I thought. 'You can talk to a room full of teachers but you can't…'

That was about as far as the thought went. The key word was *talk*. Which led me to, 'Write it as if you were speaking it out loud!' which led me to finishing the first draft in one day. I went on to write more articles for Helen, and after I'd joined the Writers' Guild (more on the advantages of that later) I also contributed pieces to *UK Writer*.

Now there are three important points here:

1 Article writing didn't get in the way of my other work.

2 My prose style improved.

3 As a direct result, I gained in confidence and my weekly word count went up.

Find a magazine publisher

If you simply type 'freelance article writing' into your search engine, you'll get dozens of results. I know. I've just done it. So narrow your search. What really interests you? What are you passionate about?

Once you've decided, search the Internet for magazines that publish articles on that subject. Once you've found one, find their submissions policy. They'll vary. Some accept unsolicited work. Some don't. Some want to read finished articles. Some want a proposal – that is, a summary of what you want to write about. Some even pay.

Once you have found a magazine that does accept unsolicited work, read a copy and familiarize yourself with the in-house style. When you find one whose style is closest to your own, contact the editor with your idea and see if they're interested.

They may have printed a similar article to the one you're proposing six months previously and so turn you down. But you've not wasted your time. You've made contact with an editor (who may suggest a different subject for an article) and you've put forward a proposal which has at least been considered.

If they accept your proposal (and your finished article), you've made a small but important breakthrough.

There are two other things to consider:

1 The editor's decision is final, so don't argue if you get turned down.

2 You're not doing this instead of working on your book. You're doing it as well. So decide how much time you want to devote to it and pretty much stick to that. I'd suggest two weeks. Not long, I know, but, as I've already said, deadlines concentrate the mind wonderfully well.

If you're a genre writer and haven't yet joined the appropriate specialist group, do so. The journal of the British Fantasy Society (*BFS Journal*), for example, accepts unsolicited work. You might also want to have a look at *Freelance Writers News* which comes out 11 times a year. At the time of writing, a year's subscription is £29. In it there are details of various writing competitions and a letters page, but what it mainly consists of is the contact details of magazine editors and the kind of work they're looking for. See www.writersbureau.com for further details.

Storytellers and storytelling

A few years ago I worked for an agency that booked me into schools. Mainly, I was performing poetry and helping children write their own. One school asked if I'd go into Reception and tell the children a story. I was happy to agree. All they wanted me to do was sit in a room full of four- to five-year-olds and tell them the story of Goldilocks and the Three Bears. How hard could that be?

I emerged 20 minutes later, a wiser man. It's not that the children were badly behaved. Quite the opposite. They were well mannered, polite and obviously bored rigid.

So what was wrong? I knew the story, so all the details were correct. They all knew the story and, at the start of the session, were obviously looking forward to hearing it again.

Over lunch I talked to their teacher, who said, 'When you tell a story, tell it as if you believe it's true.'

Now that's one of the best pieces of advice any writer can be given. If *you're* not convinced, how can you expect anyone else to be?

Over the several years that followed, I carried on visiting schools and I introduced storytelling into my repertoire. I learned by constant practice, rehearsals and, above all, by only telling stories that I liked. It was invaluable.

Find your voice

Type 'YouTube – storytellers' into your search engine. Listen to any that look interesting. When you find one that you particularly like, listen to it until you're familiar enough with the content to retell it yourself.

Don't write anything down at this stage.

If possible, record your retelling and then listen to it. Chances are, you'll hear faults, but don't worry about that because you're not finished yet.

Next, take the story you've retold and write it down from memory. Double-space it. As you're writing, try to keep in mind not just what happened, but the words you used when telling it. Try speaking each sentence or group of sentences before you write them down. By doing that, you're developing your own voice. It's not just poetry that's about sound as well as sense. Everything you write is.

When you've finished, record yourself reading the story, leave it for 24 hours, then listen to that recording. Have your manuscript in front of you. When you come across mistakes, clumsy sentence construction, long-winded dialogue, etc., pause the recording and fix it there and then. Once that section is fixed, continue.

Repeat this exercise whenever you can or, better still, make it part of your working week. Even better, make it the same part of your working week. What you will find is that, sooner or later, you'll be able to 'hear' your own voice in your head as you write.

That's your *writer's voice*. Just as the tone of your speaking voice changes depending on the situation you're dealing with, so your writer's voice will vary depending on what you're writing about. The voice I use when I'm angry, and need someone else to understand that, is not the same voice I use when I'm talking to someone who needs comforting. The tone changes but it's still my voice.

Watch out for 'cultural theft'

A lot of stories on the Internet are told by Native American, Australian and African storytellers. Please be aware that to many indigenous people their stories are both part of their spiritual as well as their cultural heritage. In plain English, please do not publish your 'version' of a traditional story from a living culture. No matter how well intentioned, unless you have permission, it's still cultural theft.

Change the point of view

Retell a story from the point of view of one of the characters, for example The Three Bears as told by Baby Bear or Red Riding Hood from the wolf's point of view. Playing the villain can be very liberating. Ask any actor.

Orson Welles once pointed out that one of Shakespeare's many strengths was that he understood that everyone has their reasons. It's something you should keep in mind.

Which 'person'?

If your book is currently written in the third person, would it work better in the first?

A writing workout

Think back to an important incident from your own past. Good or bad, it doesn't matter. All that counts is that it still affects your emotions. Set yourself a 15-minute time limit and then write down what happened, but write it in the present tense. It will make the writing all the more immediate. Don't worry if you can't remember all the details. Invent. You're a writer and that's what writers do. When you get to the end of the allotted time, stop. Please don't cheat here; otherwise the only thing you'll be doing with your time is wasting it.

There are three purposes to this exercise, all equally important:

3 It concentrates your mind. Again.

4 It gives you the direct line to that part of your mind where your creativity is waiting – it's the same place your dreams come from.

5 It will help you develop your own individual style and nurture your authentic voice.

So repeat it whenever you can. In the unlikely event you've had an incident-free life, scour newspapers and magazines and write about anything that catches your imagination. It doesn't have to be something big like a riot or disaster of some kind. In fact, I'd advise against it. Look for something small scale. I won't say any more. You'll know it when you see it.

Self-actualization and the writer's voice

I've worked as a writer in a wide variety of locations – jails, community centres, closed wards, schools – and, again and again, I saw the same pattern emerge. Individuals suffering from low self-esteem begin writing: in the course of writing they 'forget' their apparent lack of ability; they are proud of their achievement; they write more.

I compared notes with other writers. They all told similar stories and I began to wonder why. Then a few years ago I was interviewed by a transpersonal psychology student who was researching the nature of poetic inspiration for her Master's thesis. She showed me a summary of her conclusions, which included the following:

Danielle McGregor, BSc. (Hons), MSc.

'...it is possible to conclude that each of the poets is in fact engaged in an active and ongoing quest for self-actualization.'

(The psychologist Abraham Maslow (1908–70) defined self-actualization as 'The impulse to convert oneself into what one is capable of being.')

Earlier in this chapter, I pointed out that low self-esteem led to underachievement. In extreme cases this prompts a 'not worth even trying as I'm bound to fail' attitude in people. But it can also lead to 'That'll do'. Or, worst of all, a narcissism that fools the writer into thinking that they 'need not change a word'.

I doubt if any of you fall into either the first or last category. If you did, you wouldn't be reading this book. And hopefully, by now, if you ever thought 'That'll do', you've abandoned that as well. But you may be drawn to the final option, which is: 'That's the best I can do.'

It may even be true. Let's say, you've read and reread your book until your eyes ache. You've tracked down and corrected every typo. You've cut every word you don't need. You've rewritten great chunks of it and it really is the best it can be. Well, for now at any rate.

Or, you hope it is.

So, what now? Are you finally ready to go ahead and publish?

Before you take that final step, you need to do two very important things:

1 **Get your manuscript assessed.**
2 **Get it proofread.**

Find an assessment service

If you type 'manuscript assessment services' into your search engine, you'll get a lot of hits. Be aware, and beware, though. They tend to vary in price from the fairly cheap to the very expensive and there are several where the assessor charges by the hour. In the latter case, you have no idea how much your final bill will be, so if you do decide to use this process, it might be better for you to consider somebody who charges fixed fees for specific word counts.

If you simply haven't got a lot of cash to spare, then the assorted assessment services may not be an option. What you'll need, then, is a first reader. Your ideal candidate should be someone you know and trust – so no strangers you've met in Internet chat rooms, for example. It should be somebody who isn't prejudiced one way or the other. Someone who 'just loves your work' will be no good – they'll be prejudiced in your favour and almost totally blind to your faults.

So where else could you look?

Well, as I've already mentioned, I'd avoid strangers met in Internet chat rooms. I remember seeing an ad in one a few years back which read: 'Anyone out there willing to read my book and give me your opinion?'

It was a very foolish and naive thing to do. A stranger could simply download your book, change their e-mail and steal your idea. You'd have little or no proof. That's absolute worst-case scenario. Well, actually, that's more like an 'only a poet could come up with something that paranoid' worst-case scenario. The other possibility is that the person you send the book to might very well be someone with an agenda. The commonest being: 'You read mine and I'll read yours.' This is followed by completely over-the-top praise and you, of course, are expected to respond in kind.

So, what are you left with? You could decide on the cheaper end of the manuscript assessment services and raise the money. You could contact your local library and/or Regional Arts Board and see if there are any writers' surgeries available in your area. I've run a lot of these myself and the way it usually works is you bring along a sample of your writing and have a one-to-one tutorial with a professional writer. You may even find that the writer in question is willing – for a fee – to read your whole book. But don't count on it. It's more likely that they'll read the first few pages and then talk about your style and use of language. In other words, they'll tell you if they think it has readability.

That's why, for example, when you're submitting a novel to a publisher, they often ask for a summary plus the first 50 or so pages. Despite what a lot of people may think, that's generous. Just as you or I can usually tell after 50 pages or so whether or not a book has that quality, so can they. If it hasn't got that quality, then they won't recommend it for publication.

Whenever I've made that point to an aspiring novelist I've often been told, quite angrily as a rule, that 'That's just not fair because it might get better after that!' Which may be true. But shouldn't it be the best it can be right from the start?

So let's get back to your first 50 pages.

Find a writers' surgery

Type 'writers' surgeries' followed by your location into your search engine. Chances are you'll find at least one. Look at their costs and the other services they offer. For example, you may find they offer an hourly rate. One I've just found offers one-to-one at £50 an hour.

Have a close look at their tutors and, in particular, their publishing record. I emphasize this yet again because as a general rule of thumb, the best person to give you an opinion on your work is someone who has published and is able to give you an honest assessment.

You'll also find that quite a lot of writers' surgeries offer occasional writing days and/or master classes. In my experience, they're often well worth attending. Again, look at who's running the session and, even if they're working in a genre that's not your own, consider going anyway; you can still gain a lot. Besides which, if you want to be a writer, it will help cultivate your mind and add constantly to your knowledge of the craft of writing in all its aspects.

One other thing. Often, if you're working on something in a particular genre or on a very specific subject, you get blocked. Thinking you're finished because that's the best you can manage is just as much writer's block as staring at a blank screen or page without a single idea in your head. You try everything you can think of but nothing works.

Q: What do you do?

A: Something else.

I was once asked to write some 'green' poems for children. I read a lot of stuff on the environment and I read a lot of poems but not one word came. Later that same week I went to a talk in my local library on the subject of writing historical fiction. At one point we were asked to think of a character and describe their life. The speaker had also mentioned museums.

Something sparked in my imagination and, instead of a character study, I wrote a poem about a museum in the future that contains:

> *Elephant tusks, a grey seal,*
> *White snow, green fields,*
> *The Rain Forest's very last tree.*

This was followed by another eight verses.

If that was an isolated incident, it would be possible to put it down to coincidence. But the fact is, it wasn't.

However, I digress, usefully, yet again. Back to your book. If you've joined a readers' group, is there anyone there, whose opinion you trust, who might be willing to read at least some of your book and give you their thoughts as a reader?

If you're a member of a writers' group, is there anyone there you could ask?

If the answer to either of the above is yes, then approach the person in question and sound them out. If it's a reader, what you really want to know is whether the extract they looked at made them want to read more? Did they want to know what happened next? If they say yes, ask why and then listen. If they say no, ask why and take notes.

If your first reader is a member of a writers' group, then ask them the same question but also ask them to comment on your style. And, again, whatever their response is, good or bad, listen and take notes.

If you find more than one person – that is, a reader and a writer, two readers, etc. – then don't just pick one. Give them different extracts and, if they both make roughly the same kind of comments, take note. If two people tell you your book is dull, then the chances are high that it is. So don't get too angry – though you're bound to feel a bit vexed – go away and think about it. Before you do that, ask them, calmly and politely, to say why. And then thank them.

If you are told it's a well-written page-turner, ask if they'd mind reading more. If you're lucky enough to get a yes, make doubly sure they realize what's involved and have the time to do it and then await their conclusions. If your reader likes the whole book and you trust their judgement, then you might be getting close to that point when you can seriously think about publishing.

But before you do that *read it again*!

If you have the slightest nagging doubt about so much as a single sentence, read it aloud. How does it sound? Does it ring true? Remember the schoolteacher I mentioned earlier who said, 'When you tell a story, tell it as if you believe it's true.'

Jimmy McGovern, screenwriter

'My first drafts are always full of effort. With subsequent drafts I try to make it look effortless, to make it look as if I found the story in the street.'

Look at the above quotation and now think back to the other one about telling 'a story as if you believe it's true'. One is from a Reception teacher who is talking about children's stories. The other is from an award-winning screenwriter. What they're both saying is, essentially, the same thing. Whether your book is non-fiction or fiction, sci-fi, fantasy, romance or gritty social realism, does it sound true?

Is it the book you want to write or is it the one you feel that you should? Because if it's not the book you want to write, if it's not your own authentic voice speaking, no matter how many drafts it goes through, it will never be right.

If that's the case, have you wasted your time? No, of course not. In writing, nothing's ever wasted. If your book is still not right and you know it, go back and redraft. Or even start again.

The fantasy writer Nina Allan, acting on the advice of Christopher Priest who wrote *The Prestige*, redrafts by printing out her manuscript and then retyping onto the computer from scratch. In an interview in the Autumn 2012 issue of the *BFS Journal* she said:

> *...it changed my life. The improvements were vast... Writing proper second drafts – third drafts if necessary – is now an indispensable part of my writing practice, and I know that all the most sizeable improvements in my work have come about either directly or indirectly because of it.*

You could begin a rewrite with just your summary; use that as a plan and begin again from there.

You could, as I've already suggested, try retelling the story in the first person. If you do, choose the character that interests you the most, even if it's the villain of the piece. Just remember Orson Welles' dictum: Everyone has their reasons.

If you're confident that you're getting ready to publish, then in Chapter 7, we'll talk about final preparation of your manuscript.

Focus points

- Self-published books need to be a cut above when it comes to quality.
- Readers' groups are well worth joining. They provide structure, broaden your reading habits and provide you with primary-source market research.
- It's important, whether your book is fiction or non-fiction, to develop your own writer's voice because...
  - every book's a narrative *and*
  - the best way to find your writer's voice is through writing, *so*
  - widen your net and open your mind to new influences.
- Try writing in the present tense.
- When you've done all you can, get your manuscript both assessed and proofread.
- If possible, attend a writers' surgery.
- If you get writer's block, do something else for a while.

Where to next?

In Chapter 5 we look at how to publish your book the traditional way – by producing printed books.

5

Print and print-on-demand

Tom Green

The traditional method of self-publishing, paying for a run of printed books, remains a valid approach if you are confident that you can sell a large number of copies – at least 500 and perhaps as many as 1,000. If you don't expect to sell this many, then you should probably start with print-on-demand and/or e-books (see Chapter 6).

Offset printing

Offset printing is the most common method for books with a reasonably large print run. There are different types of offset printing suitable for different kinds of book. What all have in common is that the set-up costs are relatively high but the marginal unit costs (that is, the cost of printing each additional book) are low. The more copies you print in one run, the cheaper the unit cost overall (that is, the cost of each individual book).

You cannot use offset printing for print-on-demand. If you want more copies, you will need to pay for a whole new print run.

Offset printing makes economic sense only if you need a relatively high print run of at least 500, or possibly even 1,000 books.

You might not think 500 books sounds like a very large number, but most self-published books sell only around 100–150 copies.

Unless you have existing orders or a strong track record, it is unlikely that you will want to use offset printing.

Digital printing – print-on-demand

Digital printing normally has very low set-up costs, but the costs for printing each additional book will be higher than for offset printing and do not tend to fall as the print run increases.

Because the set-up costs are lower, digital printing makes economic sense for shorter print runs – fewer than 500 copies, or perhaps fewer than 1,000, depending on the book.

Digital printing also enables print-on-demand. This means that, whenever a book is ordered, a copy is printed and dispatched. The set-up costs are normally captured in the selling price (of which the printing company keeps a percentage), so as a self-publishing author you will face no up-front costs for printing.

For most self-published authors, digital print-on-demand will be the best option. If you end up selling lots of books, you can meet the demand, or, if your sales really take off, get a larger print run done through offset printing.

QUALITY

The quality of digital printing used to be much lower than offset printing or letterpress printing (which preceded offset and is still used for some limited-edition books today). These days, the quality of good digital printing is excellent. But if you are publishing high-quality images, or wish to publish to an exceptional quality, you should speak to printers about the best options, look at samples of their work and compare costs.

Evaluate possible sales

How many books will you sell? List the possible sources of sales – and be realistic. Ask others on relevant forums and social media how many copies authors of similar books have sold. Don't be misled by the few who have had bestsellers; you can learn from them but don't assume that you will be able to emulate their success.

Vanity publishing

Before the rise of digital publishing, self-publishing was blighted by so-called 'vanity publishing' companies that frequently over-charged and over-promised. Typically, they would offer a range of publishing services that they said were essential and required a much higher print run than necessary. Rather than preying on the 'vanity' of authors, it is perhaps truer to say that they were taking advantage of ignorance. Publishing can be made to seem more complicated than it really is, and the prospect of having a book in print can be a very strong incentive.

These days there is no need to pay a company to publish the book for you, even if you want to publish via an offset press. You can contact printers, find the best price and then discuss with them how you want the manuscript prepared.

Whenever you engage a company or an individual to work on your behalf, make sure you are clear what you will get for your money. Check the terms and conditions and get reliable references from other people who have used the service. If possible, contact those people yourself to ask them about the service they have received. Alternatively, ask people on relevant forums and through social media.

Shop around

The easiest way to make sure you are not taken advantage of by a printer or self-publishing company is to compare estimates from several providers. If things aren't clear, ask for more detail. And ask other people online who have been through the process for advice.

Doing it yourself

As a self-publisher you can choose how much of the process to do yourself, and how much to pay someone else to do.

It's easy to find companies that will manage everything, taking a manuscript from you and then proofreading it, preparing it for print, laying out the text, designing the cover, and either printing the number of copies you require or setting it up for print-on-demand.

If you don't want to be involved in any of that work, find a company you can trust – ideally through several recommendations. If you can afford to spend what will probably be several thousand pounds, then this can be a good option. We'll discuss self-publishing companies in more detail below.

However, if you want to save money and are happy to learn about the various parts of the publishing process, then you should not find it too difficult. There may still be professional services you choose to buy, but you can pick and choose when you need them.

The most important job for a self-publisher is to make sure that your manuscript is properly prepared for print. Some self-publishers are tempted to rush through this, keen to get on with what might seem to be the more exciting work of design, layout and print. But mistakes in the manuscript are the ones that you will regret most once your book is published. Take as long as it needs to make sure you get it right.

First things first...

You must make sure your manuscript is ready before you begin the printing process. It will be possible to make changes later, but it's much easier to make them at the outset (see Chapter 4).

Layout

For most books the layout of the text will be straightforward. Make sure you leave sufficient room for margins – you will be able to get advice on margin width from the printer or self-publishing service you work with.

Always number the pages.

There are common approaches to book layout that you will probably want to follow. There will normally be a half-title page (with just the title and nothing else), followed by a blank page and then the title page (containing the title, author, editor, edition number and publisher). This will be followed by the copyright page (with a copyright statement and ISBN number) and then others such as a dedication page and acknowledgements (although these can also come at the end).

There are good guidelines to aspects of book layout on www.thebookdesigner.com.

If you have little experience self-publishing, it is probably best to look at the layout of a successful book in a similar genre to your own. There are many ways to handle chapter headings and section breaks, and you can see them simply by looking at books. As a general rule, keep things simple. You don't want a fussy layout to get in the way of the reader's enjoyment.

Some sites such as CreateSpace provide formatted templates that you can download and insert your text into.

Look at some 'prelim' pages

Find several books similar to yours that have been published by a mainstream publisher and look at the pages that come before the main content (called the 'prelims', short for preliminary pages). There will probably be some variation – for example, some might have a page of information about the author – but they will have quite a lot in common.

Front cover design

Your book's front cover is very important, not just as a way to advertise the work's content but also to suggest its quality. A poorly designed or printed cover can strongly influence a reader's views of the text itself.

The format for your front cover design will depend on what the printer or self-publishing service requires. Some online self-publishing companies provide tools to help you with the design and formatting for the cover, while there are also numerous companies and individuals selling design services. If you do pay for front cover design, make sure that you have seen examples of the designer's work and be clear about what you expect from them. Show them the types of cover you like for books that are similar to yours, and give them a clear brief for the dimensions and format you need, including the back cover and the spine (you will need to research this first). If possible, request sketches of several ideas so that you can choose the one you like best.

It is possible to do the design yourself, especially if you keep it simple. Ask for advice on forums and via social media and be prepared to put some time into experimenting with different ideas. You will need to have some knowledge of a design tool like Photoshop (or a free equivalent such as Gimp), or else be prepared to learn. Follow instructions closely and make sure that you are accurate in your work.

If you are using an online self-publishing company, make sure that you look at their options for cover creation. The tools offered vary between companies, and it might be a critical factor in your decision about which one to use.

Remember that the cover design needs to work well when shown in a small size. People are far more likely to encounter it as a thumbnail image on a book-retailing website than they are at a bookshop, so avoid small type or intricate images. There is more on this in Chapter 7.

Formatting

Whether you are using an online print-on-demand service or a traditional printer, you will need to format your book correctly or pay the printer to do it for you.

Online services such as Lulu and CreateSpace have detailed instructions about preparing your book before self-publishing.

Though they try to make it as simple as possible, things can seem complicated if you are not familiar with the process.

You should start by asking the printer, or finding out from the self-publishing company website, exactly what the requirements are for the format of your book.

In theory, almost anything is possible. All fonts, layouts, page sizes and designs can be accommodated – as long as you set them up correctly and pay whatever they cost.

However, unless non-standard design and layout are important for your book, it probably makes sense to start with as simple a design as possible. That way, you will make the process quicker and are less likely to make mistakes.

FONT

If you use a standard font that is found on all home computers, such as Times New Roman, you will not have to pay and are unlikely to encounter formatting problems. Times New Roman is known as a 'serif' font – one that has small tails at the ends of letters. 'Sans serif' fonts such as Arial and Helvetica are plainer. It is normal practice to use serif fonts for long sections of text, as it is easier to read.

Some unusual fonts will require payment for use, and they might cause problems for your printer. If you do use unusual fonts, make sure to embed them in the pdf. Unless you have experience in this area, it is probably best to stick with one of the most common fonts. Printers and self-publishing websites will be able to tell you which fonts to use.

If you are unsure about what size font to use, ask for advice. The common sizes will vary depending on the size of the book.

PAGE SIZE

You will normally be offered a set choice of page sizes to choose from. You are likely to want the size that is most common in the market for the type of book you are writing. But you might select a size that you hope will make your book stand out. Whatever you choose, you will need to make sure that your manuscript is in roughly the same dimensions and is roughly the same size. If you are using a printer (for either offset or print-on-demand), they will probably help you with this if your manuscript isn't correctly sized. However, when working through an online company, unless you pay them to do it for you, you will need to get it right yourself. For example, if you select a book size smaller than your manuscript then everything will be scaled down in the printed book and the fonts might be too small.

Again, if you select a common size and shape and are using standard word-processing software, then this should not present any problems. Check the formatting instructions for your chosen self-publishing service and, if you have any doubts, either contact them directly or ask in one of the self-publishing forums.

In Microsoft Word you can change the size and dimensions of your manuscript using File > Page Setup > Paper Size. Other word-processing programs have similar menus.

Size (and shape) matters

Look at the books on your own bookshelves and think about the size and shape of different kinds of work. Do certain books have a certain size in common? What size and shape are most of the books that are similar to yours?

IMAGES

For most standard self-publishing services it is possible to include images in your book. However, you will need to be careful about how you present these images for print. If you are working directly with a printer, talk to them in detail about what they require. For online services, read the detailed instructions about the image size and layout requirements. For example, if you want images to be full-bleed (set to the very edge of the page), there might be certain formatting to undertake.

CREATING A PDF

Most self-publishing services will accept common word-processing files but recommend that you convert your manuscript to a pdf before uploading. This reduces the chance of formatting errors.

You can convert your manuscript to a pdf in most word-processing software by clicking on 'print' and then selecting 'print to pdf' or just 'pdf' from the printer options. Alternatively, you can buy Adobe software to make pdfs or download free software to create pdf files.

If you are making extensive use of colour and images, you should read the detailed requirements for preparing a pdf.

Self-publishing websites should have guidance about making pdfs. If you have problems, ask them or seek help via a forum or social media.

Paperback or hardback?

Unless you are publishing a book that you expect to sell at quite a high price – for example, one with high-quality images and design – you are unlikely to want your book to be hardback. The additional costs in production and distribution just won't be worth while.

WHAT KIND OF PAPER?

The quality of paper can make a big difference to the look and feel of the book, so it is worth asking to see samples if you are working directly with a printer, or ask in a forum or via social media if you are using an online self-publisher. Unless you are printing high-quality images or require premium quality, for example, for a commemorative book of some kind, then you are unlikely to want the highest-quality paper.

However, the lowest-cost options can sometimes feel cheap, so it is worth finding out more about them first.

Again, unless you are producing a premium book of some kind, you should probably use whatever the normal paper is that the printer or self-publishing service recommends. If you have photographs or graphics, seek advice about what weight and type of paper you will need.

BINDING

For paperbacks, the most common option is 'perfect binding', where the cover wraps around the pages. You might also consider 'saddle stitch', if you have a small number of pages, or 'spiral bound', if you are printing something more like a manual.

For hardbacks the binding is normally 'casewrap', which you will find used for hardbacks on your bookshelf. You will probably also have the option to put a dust jacket over that, on which the cover design is printed.

ISBN

An ISBN (International Standard Book Number) is a unique code for each book (or e-book) that booksellers or the public can use to identify it. It will normally be shown as a barcode on the back of the book.

It can be difficult to sell a book without an ISBN number as both major online retailers such as Amazon and bookshops require them. ISBNs are not always required for e-books, but if you do get an ISBN for an e-book it must be different from that used for a print version of your book.

Only one agency in each country is authorized to issue ISBNs although many self-publishing companies (including Amazon CreateSpace) will offer them to you either for free or as part of a package you purchase.

You can get more information about ISBNs and how to purchase them in the UK from Neilsen www.isbn.nielsenbook.co.uk. However, you can only buy ISBNs from Neilsen in blocks of ten, with the price currently at £121. So, unless you are planning to publish a number of books, it probably makes sense for you to get one from a self-publishing company.

The only problem with this is where you want to create your own publishing 'imprint' – that is, a brand name under which you publish. Normally, if you use an ISBN from a self-publishing company, they will be listed as the publisher. If this matters to you, then, unless the self-publishing company offers a 'custom' ISBN, you will need to purchase a block of ISBNs yourself.

Note that if you are reprinting a book without changes, then you must use the same ISBN. But if you are printing a new edition, then a new ISBN must be obtained.

Pricing

The price you set for your book will probably depend on a number of factors, including:

- what the typical market price is for this kind of book
- how much the book costs to produce
- how much money you hope to make
- how many copies you hope to sell.

It will help if you produce a simple business plan setting out your estimates relating to all of these things so that you can estimate how much money you will need to invest and how many copies you will need to sell to break even. Be realistic when you do this, basing all of your estimates on evidence rather than aspiration. Selling books is rarely easy and the market is extremely competitive.

Research the going price

Search online for books similar to your own and note down the prices. It's likely to be difficult for you to sell books that are much above the market rate, unless you have a unique proposition. Most self-published books sell fewer than 150 copies, and even this number can be hard to achieve. When estimating your sales and revenue, be realistic and try to base estimates on evidence from market research and what self-published authors of similar work have achieved.

MARKET PRICE

As a self-published author you will be in competition not just with other self-publishers but also books published conventionally. There is likely to be a typical market price in the genre your book fits into, but there will probably also be numerous discounts and special offers. Lesser-known authors might price their work lower than those who are more established, although sometimes established authors can use economies of scale (i.e. printing large numbers of books) to achieve a lower price. If the market for your book is specialized, you might be able to set a higher price. Indeed, sometimes a higher price can help establish the credibility of your book. Remember that you are also in competition, to some extent, with e-books, many of which are priced at less than a pound.

Production costs

Unless money is no real concern, keep your production costs as low as possible. With digital printing-on-demand they could be almost zero if you have expertise in book production and design or can get people to help you for free. But if you do need to pay people for things like editing and front cover design, the costs can soon mount up. With print-on-demand the costs of printing are included in the price of each book sold. Your share will be whatever is left over from the sale price once those costs are covered. Other retailers, online and offline, will have different models for pricing and payment. For offline sales you will probably need to pay to have stock printed, and it is very unlikely that retailers will pay for anything unless they are likely to sell it.

HOW MUCH MONEY YOU HOPE TO MAKE

If you are planning to self-publish a printed book to make money... good luck! The competition across the publishing industry is intense and it's very hard to break even, let alone to make money. Unless you have a proven track record, it's probably best to exercise caution at the start rather than investing large amounts of money up front. Spend what it is required to produce the book you want, and then proceed cautiously. Print-on-demand means you don't need to spend a lot, you can test the market and can respond as your sales increase. Don't be tempted to push the price of your book up in the hope that it won't affect sales – it will. Unless you have a special selling point, you are unlikely to sell many copies above the market rate.

 ## Start small

It's difficult to make money self-publishing because the market is so competitive. Be ambitious, but start small and avoid risking money you can't afford to lose.

HOW MANY COPIES YOU WISH TO SELL

For some authors it is more important to reach a wide audience than to make money. If this is true for you, then you should consider producing an e-book as well as (or instead of) a printed book, as electronic publishing offers lower prices and far easier national and international distribution. Maximizing sales will depend significantly on your marketing, the quality of your book and keeping the price down. A low price on its own will not be sufficient. There is no shortage of very cheap books and free e-books, so very few people will be tempted by price alone.

Distribution and retail

Before the widespread use of the Internet and print-on-demand, distribution was one of the biggest challenges for self-publishers. If you take an independent route and work by yourself with a printer, you will still need to overcome this. Where will you keep your stock? How will you deal with enquiries? How will you process payments? How will you distribute books? It's not impossible, but it's not straightforward, either.

Online self-publishing companies can manage most of this for you. With print-on-demand there is no need to keep surplus stock and all sales can be processed by the retailer. There are different models of distribution, so check what the different self-publishing companies offer.

Bookshops, though far less important than they used to be, can still play a part in selling your book. Local stores, in particular, can be receptive to special events and book signings. However, shelf space in the big retailers is extremely hard to obtain unless you have a proven track record and a very strong proposition.

Revisions

With print-on-demand it is normally quite easy to revise your manuscript after publication. Your book might become unavailable for sale while the new version is uploaded, but that should be the only disruption. If the changes are significant, it is normal practice to number the book as a new edition.

Self-publishing companies

Services offered by self-publishing companies have been mentioned throughout this chapter. It is still possible to do everything independently, working with freelance specialists such as editors and designers as required and then finding a printer to produce the books. But it is far from straightforward and, unless you have a particular desire to learn about and manage the entire process, you are probably better off working through a self-publishing company.

A quick Internet search will show you just how many companies there are, from big multinationals to small local companies.

Some companies focus on selling a package of self-publishing services for a fee up front. This might suit you and, once you have established the company's credibility and, ideally, heard from authors who have used them, you might be happy to pay it. However, be very clear about, what they are offering before you commit to them and be wary of additional services that make publishing more expensive than it needs to be.

Some of the best-known international self-publishing companies such as Lulu and CreateSpace don't require up-front payments. They do offer a range of editorial, design and marketing services that you can buy, but it is not required. They make their money from a proportion of the sales price of each print-on-demand copy that is sold. Lulu offers sales through Amazon, which is by far the most significant book retailer in the UK and internationally. CreateSpace is owned by Amazon, so offers the best integration with Amazon sales. Both CreateSpace and Lulu also make it easy to monitor your sales and earnings.

Services and requirements for all self-publishing companies differ, so take the time to do research and find out which one is best for you.

Tax

You are liable for tax on any profits you make selling books and e-books. All earnings must be declared as part of your tax return. Because some of the biggest self-publishing companies (notably Lulu and CreateSpace) are based in America, royalties on their sales might attract an automatic tax from the American Inland Revenue Service (currently 30 per cent). However, this is not always the case and, if you complete a W-8BEN form, which is available on self-publishing companies' websites, UK self-publishers (and those from many other countries) will be exempt from this tax on all sales apart from those that take place via American-based websites or retailers.

If you have queries about the tax treatment of your royalties, consult a tax expert, or the help section of the relevant self-publishing service.

Know what you're getting

If you spend money up front, make sure you know what you are getting in return. Take time to do research into the various different companies. Read articles online and try to make contact online with authors who have self-published with different companies so that you can learn from their experience. Bear in mind that services change and develop, so a comment or complaint made by someone a year or two ago might not still be relevant.

Focus points

- Unless you are confident of sales exceeding 500 copies, then print-on-demand will be the best option.
- Print-on-demand companies will usually also process sales and manage distribution.
- Preparing and formatting your manuscript correctly are key.
- Take time to learn about formatting and cover design, even if you then decide to pay someone to do this for you.
- Be realistic with your business plan, and don't spend more than you can afford on production in the hope that your sales will be high.

Where to next?

In Chapter 6 we explore what is today the usual option for those self-publishing – the e-book.

6

Self-publishing e-books

Tom Green

The market for e-books has grown hugely in recent years and the ease of publication, combined with the low cost of production and distribution, means that e-books are now the most common self-publishing option to take.

E-books can come in many formats, for many different kinds of devices and readers, but they are all delivered electronically rather than being printed on paper.

Why self-publish an e-book?

It has been possible for years to self-publish documents, for example in Word or as pdf files, which can be sold via email and websites, but the reading experience has been poor. Conventional computer screens, because of the technology used, are not comfortable to read for long periods, so few people chose them for book-length work, even where it was available.

The big change came with the development of e-readers designed to create a comfortable reading experience and to enable anyone to download books easily without having to worry about the technology behind them. Books were now available in formats that looked similar to the printed version, and the devices were able to store and index them effectively.

Buy an e-reader

If you haven't got some kind of e-reader yourself, buy one! It's a necessary investment to find out what the market is like, and to test the publication of your own book. If you're strapped for cash, you could buy one second-hand or, if you really can't afford it, borrow one from a friend or colleague.

The companies behind these e-readers, like Sony and Amazon, also put a huge amount of effort and money into marketing them and ensuring that popular books in all genres are available.

Thus, while some people still prefer a conventional printed book, there is no longer any stigma attached to publishing e-books, and many people prefer to read them.

A growing market

E-books are the simplest and most convenient way to self-publish and the market is growing for all types of content.

Once the e-book has been created it can be distributed more or less without any cost. Although you might have to pay the distributor in certain ways – for example, Amazon takes a share of each sale – there are no printing or postage costs, so publishing for e-books is much cheaper than for conventional books.

Another advantage is that you can update a text and republish it. This can cause complications and confusion if you do it too frequently, but if new information comes to light it is relatively easy to publish an updated edition, whereas in conventional publishing (although not print-on-demand) you would have to wait until the first print run has been used up.

Perhaps most importantly for the self-publishing author, especially those without a track record, e-books are the most dynamic sector of publishing. There are numerous Internet forums discussing the process and the works themselves, and the market, while extremely competitive, is also more accessible than for print books. You might choose to set your price very low or even at zero to start with, but you should be able to find people willing to sample your work and say what they think about it.

There are still traditionalists among readers, authors and publishers who think that a book is only a real book if it is made from ink and paper. But for everyone else, even if you also choose to publish a hard copy, the e-book offers an exciting and accessible way to bring your work to the widest possible audience.

What are the main formats for e-books?

AMAZON KINDLE

Although e-books look quite similar on different readers, they use a variety of formats. Requirements for different readers change as new products develop, so you will need to check the relevant websites before uploading.

The most popular e-book reader is the Amazon Kindle. You can now publish to Kindle, using Kindle Direct Publishing from Microsoft Word (doc or docx), HTML, Mobipocket (MOBI), ePub, Plain Text, Rich Text Format and Adobe pdf.

However, for best results they recommend that you upload from HTML. You should be able to convert most documents from Word (or a similar word-processing program) into HTML quite easily, but to ensure best results follow the detailed instructions outlined at a specialist website (for example http://kindleformatting.com). This will help strip out some of the excess code included in Word files that might otherwise spoil the layout when you publish to Kindle.

If your HTML content contains images or other files, they need to be saved separately in a single .zip file with no sub-folders. You should follow the detailed instructions for this on the Kindle website.

If you are familiar with HTML, you will be able to add certain HTML tags. Amazon recommends that you use only the supported tags rather than stylesheets and other formatting that the Kindle reader might not support.

If you have problems converting to HTML, it's probably easiest to upload direct from Microsoft Word or, if you don't have Word, the simplest option is to save it as a text file.

Always check the formatting of the new file before you upload it. For example, saving a Word document as a text file will remove much of the formatting, so you might need to add it to the document.

There is a maximum size for a file you can upload (currently 50MB). A text file is unlikely to exceed this amount, but if you have a number of images you might need to reduce their size or compress them to make the files smaller.

KINDLE FIRE

In 2011 Amazon launched Kindle Fire, a colour version of the e-book reader with a multi-touch screen and Android operating system that makes it, in some respects, a competitor of the iPad. Kindle Fire uses a publishing system called Kindle Format 8 that allows for a far greater flexibility in formatting and layout.

To publish for Kindle Format 8, it is recommended that you start with a Word file, follow the detailed formatting instructions and then convert the file to HTML or HTM. For more information, search online for 'Kindle Format 8' or download the free ebook 'Building Your Book for Kindle' available from Amazon.

The sales process for Kindle Fire is the same as for the conventional Kindle.

KOBO

The Kobo reader was introduced after the Kindle, but has significant support from certain publishers and retailers. Their publishing system is called Kobo Writing Life and it supports uploads in Microsoft Word (doc or docx), OPF, HTML, Mobipocket (MOBI), ePub, Plain Text, Rich Text Format and Adobe PDF.

Whichever format you upload in will be converted to ePUB. Therefore, Kobo recommends that, if possible, you upload an ePub file or an OPF file because this will result in the cleanest and most accurate conversion to the Kobo reader. If you use Apple's Pages software, you should be able to save a file directly to ePub format. However, it's not straightforward if you are using Microsoft Word (although you can download converter programs).

If you aren't able to convert your Word document to OPF or ePub format before uploading, follow the tips to formatting Word documents in the 'Uploading' section of the Kobo user guide. This will help ensure that the finished ePub file looks as close as possible to how you would like it. This includes guidance on how to format images that appear alongside the text.

A video about uploading to Kobo along with frequently asked questions and the Kobo user guide are available for free at https://writinglife.kobobooks.com/learningCentre.

Research your target audience

Contact at least ten people who might be a target audience for your book (by e-mail, on Twitter or Facebook), to ask which e-readers they have and what were the last three e-books they downloaded. Ask them roughly what they would expect to pay for a book of the type you are publishing. Although it's a small sample size, this research is still worth doing – the more you can talk to your potential audience the better.

APPLE IBOOKS

You can self-publish e-books for Apple devices, including iPad, through Apple's iBookstore. Before you start you will need to create either a Paid Books Account, which allows you to sell books and offer them for free (and for which you will need to provide banking and tax information), or a Free Books Account, if you are only going to give books away. A Free Books Account cannot be converted into a Paid Books Account later on.

In order to create a Paid Books Account you need a US tax ID so that you can process sales taxes – you should be able to obtain this from www.irs.gov.

Uploads for iBooks can only be done as ePub files – as mentioned above, these are relatively easy to create from Apple word-processing software but you will need to search for a convertor to download if you are using other software.

Apple also offers special self-publishing software called iBooks Author, which creates books in what it calls Multi-Touch format. This has a particular focus on creating text books but can be used for any book, offering templates and tools to create extra functionality within the book that can help make the most of the interactivity available to iPad users. However, if you publish from iBooks Author you can only distribute the book (in any form) through Apple devices.

The iBookstore works through Apple's iTunes system, so if you do not already use this, or have an Apple ID from elsewhere, you will need to download iTunes to get an ID. You can do this for free. For more information, see: www.apple.com/itunes/content-providers/book-faq.html

NOOK

The Nook e-reader, distributed by the American bookseller Barnes & Noble, was first sold in the UK in 2012. Its market share in this country is still small, but it has had considerable success and backing from major publishers in the US.

The publishing system for Nook is called Nook Press (replacing their previous system, PubIT!). Uploads can be in ePub, Microsoft Word, HTML or text. For more information and updates about using the system in the UK, visit www.nookpress.com.

GOOGLE PLAY AND GOOGLE BOOKSTORE

Most devices running the Android operating system can download the Google Play Book Application, which will give them access to the Google Bookstore (also accessible through a web browser on any device) containing a huge range of out-of-copyright books that Google has scanned, digitized and made available online. Content can also be transferred to many other devices, including the Nook and Sony Reader. Current books are also available for sale and for free and it is possible to submit your own printed work to be digitized or to publish an e-book.

Once you join the Google Books Partner Program – there is no fee but you must agree to the terms – you can send either hard copy or digital content of published books to be displayed in-part online with a link to other retail sites. You can also sign up for a share of the Google Ads revenue generated by pages featuring your work.

You can also upload e-books for sale via the Google Bookstore. Again, you must join the Google Books Partner Program and the section specific to e-books. You will then be able to upload your work in either pdf or ePub format. The formatting for the reader is likely to be much better if you use ePub.

OTHER DEVICES

You can publish an e-book in some format to almost any kind of electronic device, even if it is just as a pdf. They key thing, as with the systems outlined above, is to check the format requirements and seek support if you get stuck. There are also a number of services, often called aggregators, which manage the publishing process for you. Some devices, such as the Sony eReader, require you to publish through an aggregator.

Use the right formatting

You must format your work correctly before uploading. Take time to read the detailed user guide and preview your work before publishing it. Even though you can make corrections later on, it creates a bad impression if you have errors at the start. If you find formatting difficult, keep it as simple as possible in your original text.

How I do publish through an aggregator?

Aggregators are online services that help you publish and distribute your e-book. Some of the main ones are:

- Smashwords
- BookBaby
- Lulu.

These sites have a similar uploading process to those outlined above, and then export your work into a format that will work on various devices. For example, Smashwords supports distribution to Apple iBookstore (in some countries), Barnes & Noble, Sony, Kobo, Baker & Taylor, Diesel and Page Foundry.

Some, like Smashwords, take no fees up front, but take a royalty on sales; a royalty is also taken by the online retailer. You will need to work out whether this represents good value for your e-book. Others, like BookBaby, take a fee up front to help you self-publish but do not take royalties.

How are e-books sold?

Unlike conventional books that can be bought and read by anyone, e-books are often dependent on specific devices. This is partly for technical reasons as different devices use different formats and it's not possible to move content from one to another. It is also because the manufacturers of the devices tend to want to keep sales of e-books created on their publishing platform within their own systems so that they can take a share of any sales.

It's a similar concept to print-on-demand books – you tend not to pay anything up front, but give a share of any sales to the vendor. This works differently for the different devices, and you will need to decide which gives you the best deal.

In general, there is nothing to stop you publishing the same content on different e-book platforms for different devices. It's just a case of you taking the time to format and upload them, and then managing your various accounts.

Another possibility is to publish for one of the major platforms and then also create a pdf file that people without that device can buy from you directly – perhaps from your website using an online payment system such as PayPal. You are unlikely to generate many sales, because buying pdf files has not tended to be popular with readers, but it would allow anyone with a strong desire to buy the book, but without a device to read it in the format you have chosen, to buy a copy.

Perhaps the most important decision you will make is how much to charge for your e-book, although the different platforms might impose their own restrictions. You are usually able to change the price after publishing whenever you wish.

Research your competitors

Visit the Kindle bestsellers list in the category of e-books you are working on. Ignoring those by famous authors, what stands out about the successful books? Do certain themes predominate? What about cover designs? You don't have to follow what other people do but it's helpful to know what can succeed.

AMAZON KINDLE

The greatest benefit of publishing for Kindle is the easy access to a listing on the Amazon website, the largest e-book retailer in the world. It has an excellent search function and allows considerable user interaction.

Their standard royalty payment in the UK is 70 per cent of the cover price (they keep the other 30 per cent), but to qualify for this the list price must be at least 20 per cent below the lowest price for the printed book (if there is one). Amazon sets a minimum and maximum price, and there is also a 35 per cent royalty option for certain circumstances – for example, if you are publishing a book already in the public domain or if you want to set a very low sale price.

After a process of review by Amazon your book will then be made available in the Amazon store and will be available to purchase. Royalty payments will be made to your account.

The only way that you can set a price of zero, which some e-book authors do for a period of intense marketing to generate reviews and interest, is by joining the Kindle Direct Publishing Select scheme. Joining will enable you to enroll in the Kindle Owners' Lending Library – and receive royalties for loans taken out – and take part in free promotions. There is no cost, but you must commit to publishing a given e-book only through Kindle Direct Publishing and not on another platform.

KOBO

Kobo e-books are sold through its own website bookstore and, perhaps more significantly, through a series of retail partners. The most important of these in the UK is WHSmith, although the scale of stock and sales is far smaller than for Amazon Kindle e-books.

Pricing and royalty payments for Kobo are along very similar lines to the Kindle. There are minimum and maximum prices and a main royalty rate of 70 per cent. As with Kindle, payments are made directly into your account and VAT payments are processed for you.

APPLE IBOOKS

iBooks are sold through Apple's iTunes – an application with a national and global reach comparable to Amazon, although not yet as well established for books and e-books. E-books bought in the iBookstore can be downloaded and read on any Apple device belonging to the purchaser.

Remember that before you can sell books through iBookstore, you need to get a US tax ID from www.irs.gov. You can go through one of the aggregator services, which should take care of this for you.

Pricing and royalty payments and arrangements through iBookstore are normally in line with those for Kindle and Kobo.

NOOK

Royalty payments for Nook sales are generally 65 per cent of the sale price, or 40 per cent for books sold at low prices. Books are sold mainly through the Barnes & Noble website which is well known in the US but doesn't have the same profile in the UK.

GOOGLE PLAY

If you sell e-books through Google Play, you will, under normal circumstances, receive a royalty payment of 52 per cent of the cover price. This is considerably lower than other major online retailers and, if it does not change, you might want to consider whether it is worth while for you. Google Play does have a huge potential market, however.

SONY eREADER AND AGGREGATORS

The Sony eReader has an online Reader Store for sales of eBooks, but the publishing process is required to take place through aggregators such as Smashwords and Author Solutions. Most aggregators pay higher royalties than standard on sales from their own sites and slightly lower on sales through other sites. Their services, terms and conditions vary so you will need to check the details carefully.

How do you decide which format and platform is right for you?

The choice of which platform and device to choose for your e-book will probably depend on which one you think will lead to most sales. For standard e-books Amazon Kindle has by far the greatest market share and the Amazon website is a dominant force in e-books retail. They offer good support and there is the large and vibrant online community discussing and promoting their e-books. The widely used Kindle App also makes your work available on a wide range of devices, not just the Kindle.

The biggest danger is probably that of being lost amid the sheer number of titles, but unless you have a built-in preference for a niche product you would need a good reason to choose another device for your e-book.

The role of WHSmith in selling Kobo devices and titles might influence you. If you think your e-book will appeal to the Smith's audience – and, therefore, the retailer might even choose to promote the title – then they would be worth considering.

Google Bookstore will certainly be hard to ignore, simply because of Google's huge reach across the UK and the world. But the uploading process is a little more difficult to follow than with the other major sites and, most importantly, the royalty payment is considerably lower.

The Apple iBookstore is likely to be tricky for those who are not already familiar with Apple products and services. If you are, then the big appeal of publishing an iBook is likely to be its reach across the iTunes store – and the reach to that market – and the ability for your e-book to be downloaded to a variety of Apple devices. If you want to add richer content to your e-book such as graphics, animations, high-quality images, and so on, then the iBook is probably the best option, especially given that you can download and use iBooks Author for free.

Another option for richer content and greater functionality is to upload for the Kindle Fire. There is no iBooks Author equivalent but the publishing system it uses works with Word documents if you follow the formatting instructions. Kindle Fire sales are a small fraction of those enjoyed by the iPad, but it is growing in popularity and would be worth investigating if your book requires richer content than just text.

Using aggregators is probably best if you find the process of self-publishing an e-book complicated or time-consuming and prefer the idea of someone doing it for you in return for either an up-front fee or a share of your royalties. They should also ensure that you get your e-book across a number of formats and devices.

If you do favour Amazon Kindle, then the big question you will face is whether to sign up to their Kindle Direct Publisher Select scheme – to do so brings advantages in terms of flexibility of pricing but means that you must agree not to publish the work on any other platform.

How much technical knowledge do you need?

It's impossible to explain the e-book publishing process without using some technical language. As mentioned above, if you find that off-putting then you can opt to pay (via an up-front fee or a share of royalties) to get parts or all of the process done for you.

However, if you can get past any unfamiliar language, the various processes should be relatively easy to understand. The main technical requirement is the formatting. It's worth spending some time trying to get your file in the format the publisher prefers – if you get stuck, seek help from one of the many self-publishing online communities. Even though most devices support a variety of formats for uploads, the danger is that there will be formatting errors.

These can also be avoided simply by following the instructions in the relevant user guide. Both Kindle and Kobo have particularly clear instructions about formatting that do not require any real technical understanding except when it comes to HTML. Indeed, working with HTML is probably the one area that does require some specialist knowledge and you should consider doing some background work or seeking specialist help if your e-book has layouts or functionality that require accurate HTML.

What help is available – free and paid for

The best sources of help are the sites where you are uploading your e-book, but the processes change and the sites can be a little complex so take your time to navigate the relevant sections of the site and to read the user guide.

You will also find numerous articles online and videos on YouTube explaining each step of the process.

Weigh things up carefully

As well as choosing the device that best suits your work, you should choose the one with the most appropriate market. Amazon's Kindle is the dominant e-reader, but the iPad and Kindle Fire are gaining popularity and other devices also have factors in their favour. You can publish for more than one device unless you sign an exclusivity agreement.

Social media and discussion forums can also be a huge help – just make sure before posting a question in a forum that you have searched that forum to see if the question has already been answered.

If you are prepared to pay for help, then you will find a range of companies and freelancers advertising online to help with each part of the process. Before paying someone, try to understand as much as possible about what you want them to do, what the desired outcome is and what you will pay them. Get references if possible and perhaps discuss what you are planning for in a discussion forum to see what other more experienced self-publishers think.

Many of the e-reader self-publishing websites list companies that can help you through the process, and they might even offer their own service.

Uploading isn't as hard as it seems

Don't pay a freelancer or company to upload your text until you have tried yourself. The instructions can seem daunting and complicated but online self-publishing systems have been designed for users without technical experience. If you follow the instructions carefully, you should be fine.

How do you design and lay out an e-book?

The basic layout for an e-book does not vary much. The key thing is to get the formatting correct before you upload so that you do not get errors. However, for more sophisticated multimedia devices like the iPad and Kindle Fire, you can use a variety of templates to vary the design.

AMAZON KINDLE, KOBO AND OTHER TEXT E-READERS (INCLUDING FOR GOOGLE BOOKSTORE)

If you are able to upload and tag html files, then you will be able to select some simple styles covering elements such as fonts, heading styles and page breaks.

If you are uploading from Word or ePub, most simple formatting should be retained, especially if you follow the detailed instructions on the relevant device website. Most e-readers will support a range of fonts and you should be able to use different styles of headings.

Pdfs might give problems, depending on how well the site is able to convert them. Sometimes, for example, the text uploaded from a pdf will not 'flow' in the e-reader, but remain as fixed pages.

For your first e-book, however, it is probably best to keep the formatting as simple as possible or else to seek specialist help. Otherwise, be prepared to spend plenty of time researching online as you encounter a variety of formatting problems once your text is converted.

Bear in mind that there are now many different versions of each of these devices, with more new ones in the pipeline, and the functionality for each will vary. While you can use a preview tool before you publish, it probably also makes sense to try something relatively simple first of all so that you can see it published on different versions of the chosen device.

Although some e-readers automatically skip past the front cover, it is still an important part of the design of your e-book. It is what readers are likely to see in publicity and listings, and it therefore needs to give them a clear idea of what your book is about.

The user guides for different devices explain very clearly how to upload your front cover artwork, and the restrictions in terms of size and colour.

Most of the self-publishing systems make it relatively easy to change the cover at any point. You can also change the text and some – for example, Amazon – offer to email everyone who has bought the book with any significant updates.

iPAD AND KINDLE FIRE

Layout and design for devices with more interactivity, such as the iPad and Kindle Fire, can also be kept simple if your e-book is primarily text. If you want to make more of the functionality they offer, then the process is more complicated. Both of these devices offer systems to make it easier for non-HTML specialists (iAuthor for iPad, Word documents with KindleGen for Kindle Fire), but you will still need to develop some knowledge of design and layout if you are to make the most of what's on offer.

Again, it probably makes sense to start with something relatively simple and then gradually build and develop your expertise.

What are the different processes for publishing an e-book?

The publishing process for most e-readers is relatively similar and quite straightforward. The user guides will take you through step by step, including with regard to the following aspects:

- **Formatting your text** As discussed above, this really is the key step!
- **Confirming rights and suitability** You must own the rights for whatever you publish in all the territories in which the e-book will be published. The self-publishing site from which you upload will explain which these will be. Your work will also need to conform to the terms and conditions regarding things like explicit images and libel. Again these will be set out as you go through the self-publishing process.
- **Entering title and summary** These are required for the book listings on the relevant sales websites.
- **ISBN details (if you have them)** An ISBN (International Standard Book Number) is a unique code for each book (or e-book) that booksellers or the public can use to identify it. Not all e-retailers require an ISBN: Amazon does not, for example. If you choose to get an ISBN it must be different from that used for a print version of your book. Unfortunately you can only buy them in blocks of ten, with the price currently at £121.

Remember...

Remember, you can get more information about ISBNs and purchase them from www.isbn.neilsenbook.co.uk.

- **Select pricing and royalty levels** – and confirming bank and tax details if your e-books are for sale.
- **Uploading your text (and pictures)** – with the opportunity to review and make changes before it is published.
- **Publishing your e-book** There will normally be a period of review before the work is available for sale.

Tax

You are liable for tax on any profits you make selling e-books. All earnings must be declared as part of your tax return. Because some of the biggest self-publishing companies (notably Lulu and CreateSpace) are based in America, royalties on their sales might attract an automatic tax from the American Inland Revenue Service (currently 30 per cent). However, if you complete form W-8BEN – which is available on the self-publishing companies' websites – UK self-publishers, and those from many other countries, will be exempt from this tax on all sales apart from those that take place via American-based websites or retailers.

If you have queries about the tax treatment of your royalties, consult a tax expert or the help section of the relevant self-publishing service.

 Focus points

- Research the different e-readers available and decide which one best suits your work.
- You will not have to make payments up front unless you choose to contract a company or freelancer to publish your work for you.
- The standard royalty payment is about 70 per cent of the sale price.
- You can publish for more than one e-reader, unless you sign an exclusivity agreement, but you will need to upload your work in a variety of formats.
- Rich content with images and interactivity works well on more sophisticated devices like the iPad and Kindle Fire.

Where to next?

In Chapter 7 we will look at some of the finer points of publication.

7

Publication

Kevin McCann

Up to this point you've researched, written (or vice versa), redrafted, proofed, redrafted again and maybe even made a decision regarding your preferred publishing package. Now it's at this point that mistakes most often get made. After all, you're almost finished, aren't you? There's the cover, title, blurb and author biography left to do, but you can rattle through those in a couple of hours. In a day at the most!

Well, no, actually – now read on.

Before you take the final step and publish your book, you'll need to ask yourself some crucial questions:

- Am I satisfied that this book is the best it can be in terms of content?
- Has it been carefully and accurately proofread to the point where there are no obvious typos, grammatical or punctuation errors?
- Do I have any nagging doubts lurking in my mind?

If the answer to all three is an honest (as opposed to a wished-for) yes, then we're ready to proceed.

Tom touched on cover design in Chapter 5 but there are also other things to consider:

- the title
- the contents page
- the blurb
- the author biography.

Title

This is often the last thing to be chosen. If you still haven't thought of a title that you like, don't worry about it. Give your book a working title, for example *My Novel*, and turn your mind to something else. Keep a notebook and pen or an iPad – whichever you prefer – with you at all times and jot down anything that comes to mind.

Never assume that you'll remember a possible title and be able to write it down when you get home. You may not. Besides which, you're a writer, *so write*.

A lot of writers use quotations from other works for titles, for example:

- *Something Wicked this Way Comes* by Ray Bradbury (*Macbeth*)
- *The Mirror Crack'd from Side to Side* by Agatha Christie ('The Lady of Shalott').

Or they'll take a well-known rhyme:

- *Tinker, Tailor, Soldier, Spy* by John Le Carré (seventeenth-century nursery rhyme)
- *All the King's Men* by Robert Penn Warren (nineteenth-century nursery rhyme).

You'll have noticed that John Le Carré has changed the quotation slightly, replacing 'Sailor' with 'Spy'. Ian Fleming did something similar when he took part of the old adage 'You only live once so make the best of it' and altered it to get *You Only Live Twice*.

Another way is to take the name of your central character and make that the title, for example:

- *David Copperfield* by Charles Dickens
- *Doctor Zhivago* by Boris Pasternak.

Or take the central character's name and combine that with the theme of the book:

- *Alice in Wonderland* by Lewis Carroll
- *Harry Potter and the Philosopher's Stone* by J.K. Rowling.

Or zero in on the theme of the book:

- *Catch-22* by Joseph Heller
- *The Hound of the Baskervilles* by Sir Arthur Conan Doyle.

Or even its geographical location:

- *Salem's Lot* by Stephen King
- *Wuthering Heights* by Emily Brontë.

The variations are endless but in the end what you're looking for is a title that's eye-catching. You'll know it when it comes to you. Just don't settle on the first thing that does. When you think you've picked a title, check on the Internet and make sure no one else has used it recently.

Two last points on titles before we move on. In non-fiction it has become the norm to keep it simple and fairly obvious. Charlie Chaplin's autobiography was called *My Autobiography;* Stephen Hawking's history of time was called *A Brief History of Time* ... and so on. But it's not legally binding.

George Orwell's report on poverty in 1930s north-west England was called *The Road to Wigan Pier;* Laurie Lee's account of his travels in Spain during the build-up to the Civil War was called *As I Walked Out One Midsummer Morning.* The title comes from the first line of an old folk song 'The Banks of Sweet Primroses'. Both are intriguing titles and, in my opinion, a lot snappier than *Poverty in 1930s Lancashire* or *My Travels in Pre-Civil War Spain.* So, if your book is non-fiction, try to sidestep the obvious.

If your book is a collection of short stories, consider taking the title of the strongest story in the collection and making that your title.

Contents

Will your book have a contents page? Does it need one?

Well, again it depends on the kind of book you've written. In non-fiction it's not only the norm, it's common sense. If you pick up a history, you'll want to know what it covers and where, in the book, it is covered. Ditto for biographies, science books, memoirs, and so on.

On the other hand, if it's a novel, unless your chapters have titles, why do you need to list them?

However, if your book is short stories, you may want to include a contents page.

 ## Check the page numbers

If you have chosen the print-on-demand process, after you've uploaded make sure that the page numbers in your contents still match the page numbers in the book before you click Publish, especially if you have changed the page or font size.

One other thought, with regard to short stories. How have you decided on the running order? One tip I was given concerning poetry collections – and which I know from experience also applies to short stories – is to begin with a strong story and end with the best one in the collection.

 ## Save the best until last

In a collection of short stories, never begin with your best story – the rest of your book will feel like an anti-climax.

When James Joyce put together *Dubliners*, he began it with 'The Sisters', which concerns a recent death, and ended it with 'The Dead', which also concerns a death but not so recent. It's not only a strong story, but it ends with this astounding passage:

> '...*snow was general all over Ireland. It was falling over every part of the dark central plain, on the treeless hills, falling more softly upon the Bog of Allen and, farther westward, softly falling*

into the dark mutinous Shannon waves. It was falling too, upon every part of the lonely churchyard on the hill where Michael Furey lay buried. It lay thickly drifted on the crooked crosses and headstones, on the spears of the little gate, on the barren thorns. His soul swooned slowly as he heard the snow falling faintly through the universe and faintly falling, like the descent of their last end, upon all the living and the dead.'

Now that may be the best last page I've ever read. Try it for yourself. Read it out loud and you'll see what I mean.

Another approach that's sometimes possible is chronological. Put simply, if you have stories set in different time periods, begin with the one furthest back in history and work forward to the present; or begin with the present and work backwards; or group the stories thematically; or if they're a mixture of very serious, semi-serious and humorous try alternating – for example, precede a very serious story with something humorous and follow it with a semi-serious story.

Again, the variations are endless.

One other tip: if you've done all that and yet… try taking the first and last stories in the book and swapping them round. To be honest, I've no idea why this works but I know it often does.

Front cover

As Tom mentioned in Chapter 5, some publishing companies provide tools to help you design a cover and/or offer a choice of generic covers – that is, something eye-catching but not specific. So you might get a cover with two colours, the title, your name and the whole thing edged with a simple design.

Or, of course, you can pay someone to do it for you, but, again, as Tom has pointed out, you could end up with a bill that runs into thousands. Now, if you can afford to do that and want to, go ahead.

However, if you either can't afford it or simply don't want to spend more on the cover than you have on the book, then there are a number of alternatives.

You've already looked at book titles, now have a look at their covers.

- Which ones catch your eye and, more importantly, why?
- Which ones don't you like and, even more importantly, why?

You need to know not just what you like (and why) but also what you don't like (and why). You've got a critical faculty which you can apply to writing. You can also use that same faculty to think about graphic art. And let me be really clear here. Whatever image you decide on, it must be something appropriate but it must also be something you like. So you don't have to pick the kind of image everyone else is choosing.

Three quick points to note here:

1 **By all means be inspired by what you see but never just take a design from somewhere else. It's an infringement of copyright.**

2 **Always check that an image you've found on the Internet is in the public domain. Don't just assume it is.**

3 **Never use clip-art: it will make your cover look cheap and therefore sends out the wrong message.**

So, where does that leave you?

Well, maybe what you need is an image that is original to you and therefore not infringing anyone's copyright. One obvious solution is to do it yourself.

If you've looked at lots of different book covers, you could be forgiven for thinking that, unless the cover is artwork, it won't do. That's simply not true. Let me explain. Whether you go for print-on-demand and/or e-publishing, the cover is the first thing your potential readers will see when they go on to your sales page. The cover consists of a design plus title and your name. We've already talked about the importance of finding a good title that catches the eye. The same applies to your cover design. And just as a book is either well written or badly written and that's all, so a design is either eye-catching or it isn't.

It doesn't matter whether it's a photograph, line drawing or painting, collage or abstract. All that matters is that it's right for your book.

So, to begin with, you need to think about your book's theme. What's it about? How would you sum it up? *Call of the Wild* by Jack London, for example, is about the wolf that is buried inside every domesticated dog. Now, take that sentence you've just read. Does it suggest an image to you?

Developing cover designs

Either write a brief description of a cover design for *Call of the Wild,* or draw it or Photoshop it. It doesn't matter if you haven't read the book – although, if you haven't, I recommend that you do. What we're thinking about here is imagery. What we're looking for, specifically, is one image that suggests an entire book. Notice I said 'suggest' there and not 'summarize'. How could you summarize *Oliver Twist* in one image? You can't but you can suggest it by using an image that's now so well known, it's almost a cliché.

Let's take two more very well-known titles:

- *Dracula* by Bram Stoker: the first images that will spring to most people's minds are: old castle; man in an opera cape; male/female vampire lying in a coffin.
- *Frankenstein* by Mary Shelley: old castle/tower and lightning; mad scientist and/or monster.

Now think of two images, one for each book, that suggest the story but don't use any of the elements I've listed. Again, don't worry if you haven't actually read them. If you type 'Dracula by Bram Stoker – Wikipedia' into your search engine, you'll get a summary of the plot. The same applies to Mary Shelley's *Frankenstein*.

Try repeating this exercise using other books you're familiar with. In each case, ask yourself 'What is this book's theme?' and then take it from there.

Finally, go back to your own book and repeat the exercise as many times as you need to until you come up with an image that:

- fits in with your book's theme *and*
- you can produce using either original artwork or a photograph.

Don't just settle on the first thing unless you're absolutely head over heels in love with it. Each time you do this exercise, the image that is perfect for your book will become more and more clearly fixed in your visual imagination. The exercise is like a lens bringing a blurred picture into sharp focus.

Think photographs

And, as I keep saying, your cover and title will be the first thing your
potential readers will see. If it's your first book and you're not yet a
'name', it must have something that makes it stand out from all the
others in your field.

Once you know the type of image you want, go out looking for
it. Get yourself a digital camera and start taking photographs. But
remember, you're not just looking for a good image, you're looking
for a good image that fits your book. If it doesn't, you might as
well have saved yourself the bother and just used one of the generic
images provided by a self-publishing company.

There's something else to consider. If your book is set on the coast, then
a photograph of the sea is perfectly acceptable. If it's about a horse,
then a photo of a horse will do nicely. But, again, you can sidestep the
obvious and go for an image that suggests something in itself.

I've got a copy of *The Spy Who Came in from the Cold* by
John Le Carré whose front cover consists of a black-and-white
photograph of a man in a long coat and wearing a trilby standing
on a small jetty, looking out to sea. He has a briefcase and there
are seagulls flying all round him.

It's an evocative image and suggests a story in itself. In other words,
it would work as an image on its own. So aim for that.

If you've decided on one image and then see something else that
grabs your eye, give it serious thought, even if it's nothing like the
image you originally had in mind. The best ideas frequently spring
out of an intuitive leap of imagination.

Become visually literate

The blurb

This is also known as the contents description. What you're aiming
for here is somewhere between 70 and 100 words that give your
readers just enough information to make them want to read
more. So, as well as looking at book covers and titles, you need to
familiarize yourself with blurbs. From there, either go straight into
writing the blurb for your own book or, just to loosen you up a bit,
try writing blurbs for books that you've both read and enjoyed.

Write a blurb

Write your own blurb, but don't worry about the word count of
your first draft. Once written, aim to get it down to no more than
100 words. Use complete sentences – no notes or bullet points – and
when you've finished, put it aside for 24 hours, then go back and
see whether you can reduce the word count even more without
losing the sense. When you've got to the point where one more
cut would begin to make your description incomprehensible, stop.

Author biography

Don't undersell yourself but don't exaggerate either and, like the
blurb, keep the biography brief and to the point. It's also worth
remembering that you don't have to include one at all. If you've set
up a website, you may just want to put the link to the biography in
brackets after your name.

So, can I publish now... please?

Well, the short answer is 'Yes, of course you can!'

The sensible answer, however, would be 'Not quite yet... Let your first reader(s) have a look and get their opinion.' What you want to know specifically is whether the cover is eye-catching and/or the blurb arouses their curiosity. As always, listen without interruption or prejudice. In short, listen to what they've got to say and don't get annoyed if they're not keen. Because if they're right and you can suddenly see they're right, they've done you a huge favour.

If you don't agree, again, there's no harm done. You've asked for an opinion but it's your book, so if you don't agree, you don't have to change anything.

One tip here, though. If someone were to say 'I think the cover's dull', ask them why. Ask them what they'd change. Note the points being made, even if you don't agree with any of them, and then sleep on it.

You may find that your design wasn't quite right but neither were their suggestions. You may also find that a solution, often involving only a small change, will then present itself which will improve your cover out of all recognition.

This is known as tweaking and it is just as important as every other phase of the writing process. After that, you can finally publish your book, get marketing and set up your website.

 Focus points

- Don't publish until you're completely happy with the content.
- Both your title and blurb need to be eye-catching and intriguing, so give them just as much thought as every other element in your book.
- Your biography should be the unvarnished truth. Don't lie or exaggerate because, when you're found out, your credibility will be shattered.
- Ask for second (and third and fourth) opinions regarding the cover, title and blurb *and then*
- Listen and take notes!

Where to next?

In Chapter 8 we will read the experiences of three authors who have self-published.

8

Case studies

Tom Green

Many self-publishing authors are generous with their time and advice. If you are new to the process, then it makes sense to learn from their experiences. In this chapter, three authors explain why they chose to self-publish and share the lessons they have learned.

Martin Cloake

Martin Cloake has self-published two mini-books in a series called Spurs Shorts *that he launched with his writing partner, Adam Powley. One is about Danny Blanchflower, the other concerns Arthur Rowe. They have also republished the first full-length book they wrote,* We Are Tottenham, *as an e-book after the rights reverted back to them.*

WHY DID YOU CHOOSE TO SELF-PUBLISH?

I'm a journalist and I've worked in production for years. I'm also interested in technology and the media business, an area I covered as a journalist. So I've been interested in and involved with new publishing platforms and methods for years. Digital publishing has changed the game in so many ways, one of which is to change the view of, and the opportunities offered by, the self-publishing route. Essentially, digital makes the whole process more nimble. The idea for the shorts series came from the kind of thing the *Atlantic Review* was doing in the US, and the *Guardian* in the UK. Those publications are mining their archives to produce collated volumes on particular subjects.

Adam and I were both published authors through the traditional print route, and we are both experienced journalists. So we had already built a bit of brand awareness, if you want to call it that.

We wondered if we could monetize some of the writing we were already doing, while at the same time building on the profile we already had. We decided to produce books of about 6–8,000 words – not long enough for a conventional book but longer than a magazine article. The Spurs Shorts idea was based around profiling famous players from Tottenham Football Club's history, but adding some original angle and analysis so readers could find out about a player and get some original, considered analysis, and access that on mobile devices or their desktop for a short read. We wanted to offer quality and originality at a fairly low price, but a price we felt reflected the effort we put in.

The longer-term aim was to build up a critical mass of titles, and possibly to branch out into other areas under the Sports Shorts branding. A lot of the ideas we have wouldn't ever be ideas you could pitch for a full book, published traditionally. So this gives us the opportunity to publish some longer-form journalism, and to potentially make some money. Hopefully, as we put out more titles, the back catalogue will continue earning. One of the beauties of digital self-publishing is that once the initial work is done, that's it – there's no stock ordering or extra effort over the normal process of publicizing the books.

My Arthur Rowe book started life as an extended piece for *The Blizzard*, a quarterly football journal. I did a deal whereby the article was available exclusively in *The Blizzard* until the next issue came out, at which time I published a slightly fuller version as an e-book, running an ad for *The Blizzard* in the book. The deal with *The Blizzard* is that writers write for free, but get a platform and any money made is redistributed according the contribution authors make if there's a surplus. Writing for something like *The Blizzard* provides a good platform, and authors always have the option to use their material how they want after first publication.

Keep your rights

Publishing a short article magazine or website can be a launching pad for a longer piece to self-publish. So make sure you keep the rights for pieces you write for other people – especially if you aren't being paid.

Publishing the full-length book was a slightly different proposition. We'd originally been published through an established publishing house. They did want to digitize the books in their back catalogue, but the offer we were made just didn't stack up. So when the rights reverted to us, we decided to self-publish as an e-book. Over the years, since the print run sold out, we'd frequently been asked if there would be a reprint, so we thought the demand might be there. For a traditional publishing house it's more of a risk to take the chance that people saying they will buy something will convert into them actually doing so. For us, it was less of a risk.

We'd already written the book, we'd already published e-books, we had established a bit of a name for ourselves. But we wanted to offer something more – to maintain brand quality. So we wrote a new foreword and reinterviewed many of the people we'd spoken to in the original book. That way we could push a quality product, and give those who'd purchased the original book something extra if they decided to repurchase.

Look after your brand

As a self-publisher you need to look after your 'brand'. Make all your books as professional as possible and try to add value when you republish, by updating content and adding extras like a new foreword.

Various options are likely to open up in the future. We want to do more short books on a greater range of subjects. Some of those, if they sell and/or attract the attention of a traditional publisher, might lead to more traditional commissions. And we've also got the option to do full-length books that are attractive to a niche market – the sort that would not stack up economically for a publisher having to commit to a print run and production costs, but which might be viable for an individual writer.

Having a production background also helped. Many writers, quite understandably, just want to write, and when the creative part is over they prefer to hand the work on to someone else. I quite like the production side too, so something that offered greater control of pretty much the whole process appealed.

HAVE YOU USED PRINT-ON-DEMAND OR E-BOOKS?

E-books seemed simpler and more direct. The short-form books are also written with a view to them being quick reads on mobile devices.

HOW MUCH DID YOU RESEARCH INTO THE PROCESS?

I've been a journalist and subeditor for over 20 years, so I know a fair bit about production techniques. Constructing an e-book is more complex than you're led to believe, but it's also a case of thinking in a different way in order to work through the process. Having to construct books in a slightly different way for different platforms is also a bit of a pain. I did a lot of research on the Web, and through face-to-face chats and e-mail conversations. The Scrivener software was really useful for organizing that research. Online communities are very useful, too.

I also did a fair amount of research on pricing, and on the tax situation with e-book royalties, which is quite complicated. Being a journalist who works in the finance field also means I'm taking in a lot of detail about all this on a daily basis, so the 'research' is actually me just being interested in and aware of what's happening in my trade.

DID YOU GET PROFESSIONAL HELP PREPARING YOUR MANUSCRIPT?

No. I didn't need to as I am a journalist and subeditor. Adam and I bounce ideas off each other, and it's great having a writing partnership where we can both be constructively blunt and honest about ideas and execution.

WHAT WERE THE MOST CHALLENGING THINGS ABOUT THE SELF-PUBLISHING PROCESS?

Adopting the different mindset required for digital as opposed to print throws up some challenges. For example, worrying about formatting concerns like widows and orphans and hanging lines is pointless when people read the pages on different-sized devices. Unless you publish in pdf format, you don't have the same degree of control over how the product is served up, because the accessibility of digital, particularly on mobile devices, is largely about the reader deciding how to read, rather than receiving what they are given. I still find it irritating that I have to compromise on some aspects of formatting, but the point is that it just doesn't matter as much.

Format your book for a mobile device

Download a free e-book to a mobile device such as a phone or tablet. Does the formatting work OK? How easy is it to read? Think about how your book formatting might need to be adapted for mobile devices, perhaps by simplifying the layout and adding more paragraph breaks.

Making sure you meet the many and complex regulations required to get an e-book published is also quite demanding, especially when many of the aggregators seem incapable of communicating in plain English.

And ensuring you don't get a double whammy on tax is also a laborious and complex process. In a nutshell, because companies such as Amazon are based in the US for the purposes of author earnings (but not, interestingly, when it comes to the company's own earnings!), earnings UK authors make through Amazon, etc., are taxed in the US, and then taxed again in the UK unless the individual applies for an opt-out. (See Chapter 6 for information on opting out.)

WHAT DID YOU LEARN?

I'm still learning. I know how to use several new bits of software, how to solve some basic problems, and most of all I'm constantly learning about good methods of marketing the content. Each book has been slightly easier than the last, as the process becomes more familiar. So I like to think I'm constantly honing my technique.

HOW DID YOU APPROACH MARKETING AND SELLING YOUR BOOKS?

I'd already done a lot of work on marketing and promoting the books I'd had published by more traditional routes. Again, my background in journalism helped, as did Adam Powley's background working for some of the big publishing houses. Many writers, quite understandably, just want to create the product and leave it to others to market. We felt we could offer a more complete package, and that's helped in our relationship with publishers. We bring a similar approach to our own books. We both use social media a lot, and the advantage of writing, as we have done, about sports and particular sports clubs means we can involve ourselves in the various online fan communities and put the word about. We also negotiate deals with various websites and magazines, providing extracts in return for a plug and link to the book.

I have a static website that I set up as a showcase that works as a kind of online CV: www.martincloake.com. I created it myself using a piece of software called Rapidweaver, which is available for about £35. I used it to find out how to put a website together. It's a time-consuming process and I wouldn't pretend to be a web designer, but I feel I know a bit more than the basics about how to put a decent site together and what works.

I blog regularly at blog.martincloake.com.

I promote all my books through the blog, and I write about sport, journalism, media and technology and occasionally a bit of music and politics. The blog started as a way of raising my profile and demonstrating what I could do when I was preparing to go freelance. There's also a line on my profile page that talks about a journalist not blogging as a bit like someone not using electricity, and I'd stick by that.

I also use Twitter a lot, again for professional purposes, but the nature of it means there's inevitably going to be some more personal stuff. Twitter is great for networking, getting information out and, if you're following the right people, for finding out about what's going on and keeping up with the latest thinking and the latest trends. I've also got a LinkedIn profile, and I knit that network of platforms together.

On Facebook I find it's harder to maintain a divide between the personal and the professional – there's a lot of 'noise' in comparison to Twitter and LinkedIn, and I don't like the way they keep changing the interface after you've set stuff up as you want it. It's also probably a product of my being from an older generation – I noticed when I was teaching how the students pretty much lived on Facebook, and use it very effectively both personally and professionally. So I'm conscious I should probably do more on Facebook, but I find it difficult to find the time or the inclination.

Give Martin a tweet!

Look at Martin Cloake's website, blog and Twitter profile. Can you see how they all connect? Is it easy to find the books he has published, their content and tone and how to buy them? Send Martin a tweet to let him know you have read this case study.

DID YOU HAVE ANY EXPECTATIONS FOR SALES, AND HAVE YOU MET THEM?

Adam and I started the e-books strand to test the water. We knew it would be a long-term project, building up a number of titles and hopefully capitalizing as the mass created its own momentum. We deliberately didn't entertain any wild ambitions about making money; we saw it as a side project. Because we both do other work, we don't have to rely on this as an income stream. That also means we don't feel the same pressure to drop the price that someone dedicating themselves to the marketplace would. We price the books based on the effort we've put in and what we think they are worth, as well as with an eye to what the market will sustain.

ARE YOU PLANNING TO SELF-PUBLISH AGAIN?

Yes. We want to expand the range of subjects we cover. We've also thought about offering to help other writers use the same concept, but that needs a bit more careful thought. And I've been (cliché alert!) toying with some ideas for a novel for a while (I'm a big reader of crime fiction) so there's a possibility there – although fiction is a whole different, er, ball game.

WHAT ADVICE WOULD YOU GIVE TO ANYONE ELSE PLANNING TO SELF-PUBLISH?

- Believe in what you're doing.
- Be honest about what you're doing and what you can do.
- Work out what you can do well yourself – you'll be surprised at what you don't need to buy in.
- Get real experts to do the stuff you can't do, for example, cover design. Amateurism doesn't sell and it doesn't promote quality. You might be able to barter expertise, but always remember you're not the only person who needs to make money.
- Be prepared to put lots of time in.
- Network, market, publicize.

Mel Sherratt

Mel Sherratt has self-published a crime thriller, Taunting the Dead, *and three books in a series called* The Estate: Somewhere to Hide, Behind a Closed Door *and* Fighting for Survival. *She has also published two other books under a different pen name.*

WHY DID YOU CHOOSE TO SELF-PUBLISH?

I tried for 12 years to get a book deal and in the past two years had an agent trying to place my books without success. So I studied the Kindle markets for a few months, watching authors such as Kerry

Wilkinson hit the top of the charts, and decided to give it a go for myself. I also knew self-published author Talli Roland who became a huge help to me. I am now mentoring two other writers in the way that she helped me.

HAVE YOU USED PRINT-ON-DEMAND OR E-BOOKS?

Primarily I use e-books but I did use print-on-demand for one of my books, *Somewhere to Hide*, because I want it to be available for people who can access a digital copy. The profit I make is minimal. The majority of my sales will always be digital, but to enable readers to purchase a print copy, which is obviously more expensive, I decided to keep my price as low as I could rather than add a couple of pounds, profit.

HOW MUCH DID YOU RESEARCH INTO THE PROCESS?

I watched the Kindle sales charts for months to see who was selling, who wasn't, what genres were selling, the prices, etc. Then I read an e-book on how to create the document and upload it on to Kindle Desktop Publishing. I worked out my own strategies and pressed upload.

Check out what's selling

Follow Mel's lead and look at the Kindle sales charts for books in your genre. Make sure you have read most of the bestsellers and have learned lessons from their content, format and design. It's also worth investigating how they have been marketed. What is it that has made them a success?

DID YOU GET PROFESSIONAL HELP PREPARING YOUR MANUSCRIPT?

I didn't pay for editing or copyediting for *Taunting the Dead* but for all books after that I paid for copyediting and then proofread it several times myself. Any book I bring out in the future will always have a professional copyedit – you can't see your own mistakes.

DID YOU MANAGE THE SELF-PUBLISHING PROCESS YOURSELF?

Yes, with a little help from my mentor.

WHAT WERE THE MOST CHALLENGING THINGS ABOUT IT?

Uploading the document and getting the formatting perfect were the most difficult. Once I'd done this the first time, it became second nature, but it is fiddly to learn to get it right. Also, ensuring that the work was to a standard where a reader would take a chance on an author they had never heard of.

A mentor is invaluable

Advice from someone who has already self-published is invaluable. See if you can find someone, through personal contacts or by asking around online, who is willing to help guide you through the process.

WHAT DID YOU LEARN?

Everything! But there's a great sense of achievement to see it all done.

IS THERE ANYTHING YOU WOULD DO DIFFERENTLY?

I'd hire a copyeditor for my first novel! I also tried various sales platforms for about six months and they were far less cost effective for the time it took to create and upload the documents to specifications, and then also to get them distributed.

Match your genre to the right platform

Which retail platforms are most worthwhile? Search around online communities and ask on social media to see which genres seem to do best on the different platforms.

HOW DID YOU APPROACH MARKETING AND SELLING YOUR BOOKS?

Before I self-published, I hosted a blog called High Heels and Book Deals and for two years I absorbed myself into indirect networking. I interviewed authors and reviewed books for publicists who I met online through Twitter, and then tweeted out the posts I did to all those involved – the author, the publicist, their agent, the publisher, etc. They in turn would retweet them. In between these posts, I wrote a few about my writing journey. I then started to attend crime festivals such as Theakstons Old Peculier Crime Writing Festival in Harrogate and Crimefest in Bristol and events like Crime in the Court. This meant I started to meet the people I'd known via Twitter, plus lots more. This all took up a lot of time – I did it for at least 20 hours a week – but it was great fun. And it gave me a good network when I came to self-publish my own work.

For this reason, and because of strong word of mouth, *Taunting the Dead* went into the top 100 after five weeks.

For The Estate series I created a new website and Facebook author page and set up a newsletter. Then I added the cover to my website one month before it was due to come out, then the prologue, the blurb and the first chapter in intervals to create a buzz. All three books came out over six months. *Fighting for Survival,* the third book, was released on 21 December 2012 and by New Year's Eve it was number one in thrillers and suspense and had sold 1,000 copies.

I have a website (www.melsherratt.co.uk) that I created myself, and I also write guest blog posts or complete Q&As most weeks. I've recently started High Heels and Book Deals up again, with different topics to cover this time.

I only use social media to interact with people and readers. I tweet out my blog posts occasionally and I have a Facebook author page to chat to my readers. I think social media is useful for helping the book to get seen but not necessarily for sales. I think word of mouth is always the best thing for that.

Give Mel a tweet!

Visit Mel's website, Twitter profile and Facebook page. Are they well connected? Do they give a clear idea of the books she publishes and how to buy them? Send her a tweet or a Facebook comment to let her know you have read this case study.

DID YOU HAVE ANY EXPECTATIONS FOR SALES, AND HAVE YOU MET THEM?

Obviously I wanted to do well, but I had no idea how quickly it would take off. *Taunting the Dead* took five weeks to get into the top 100 Kindle bestsellers. It went to number one in police procedurals, number one in thrillers and number one in mysteries. It stayed in the top 10 for four weeks, hitting its highest point at number three and stayed in the top 100 for three months. It also became one of the top ten bestselling Amazon.co.uk KDP books of 2012. I never would have anticipated that!

I've recently signed a two-book deal for world English rights with Thomas & Mercer, Amazon Publishing's mystery, thrillers and suspense imprint. The two books in the deal are *Taunting the Dead*, which will be repackaged for the US market and my new novel, *Watching over You*. Self-publishing has got me this far but it's great now to have this support. Finally, I can say those magic words: I have a book deal!

WHAT ADVICE WOULD YOU GIVE TO ANYONE ELSE PLANNING TO SELF-PUBLISH?

- Make sure the decision is the right choice for you.
- Make sure the product, because it is a product, is the best you can make it – an eye-catching cover, an intriguing blurb and ensure that the copy inside is perfect.
- Don't oversell on social media – it doesn't sell books; it only makes readers aware of them.

Olivier Nilsson-Julien

Olivier Nilsson-Julien has self-published The Ice Cage, *a Scandinavian thriller, as an e-book through Kindle Direct Publishing (KDP) and* Significant Others and Possible Selves, *an academic book on French-Canadian cinema, using print-on-demand through Lulu.*

WHY DID YOU CHOOSE TO SELF-PUBLISH?

In the case of the academic book, a top German academic publisher wanted my book in a series including world-leading scholars in the field of film and media, but they asked me to pay for a print run, which I wasn't prepared to do. And, as a freelancer, I didn't have an institution to pay for the publishing. There was also the fact that an academic career wasn't my priority. I was teaching screenwriting, creative writing and doing lots of translations. So when the publisher question dragged on too long I simply put it on Lulu. Done.

HOW MUCH DID YOU RESEARCH INTO THE PROCESS?

With the academic book I kept asking the publisher offering me the deal why they couldn't do print-on-demand. When they said they couldn't, I did some limited research online, but really I just wanted to make the book available. I had no expectations whatsoever in terms of profit – it's a very niche book. I just wanted to get it out and move on.

The thriller was a different prospect. It had been picked up by a big literary agency and I'd worked on it for considerable time, on my own and later with the advice of the agent. In spite of the agent's encouragement and ultra-positive outlook no publisher took the book. A few really liked it but passed in the end. At this stage the agent offered to publish it under her imprint. The agent had already done that with some back catalogues. I was flattered, but when I looked closer at the imprint it didn't even have a website and the covers weren't impressive. I also checked the ranking and exposure of their most successful author.

After a few weeks of reading and research I concluded that I could do just as well, while also maintaining the rights to the book, because I'd been offered a deal whereby I would sign off my rights for 15–20 years for free, with no real opportunity to break the contract in case of bad sales. I did try to negotiate, as I wanted there to be some incentive for the publisher to sell my book, but the agent insisted on getting the rights for nothing.

I felt I needed to go at it on my own, but still wasn't sure if I'd missed anything, so I did a weekend self-publishing workshop with the *Guardian*. It was brilliant and very inspiring, covering development, pitching, market positioning and practical e-book publishing.

Coming out of the workshop I felt I could do it, and it also totally freed me from the misplaced stigma of self-publishing as a form of vanity publishing. As it turns out, self-published authors often earn more than their traditionally published counterparts, especially if we're talking books of comparable quality and genre. After the workshop I also read a few books on e-publishing and marketing on Amazon. I chose to publish the thriller as an e-book because one platform was said to be more efficient in terms of rankings. I would like to offer the book as print-on-demand as well but haven't got round to it. I've been too busy with the sequel and other projects.

DID YOU GET PROFESSIONAL HELP PREPARING YOUR MANUSCRIPT?

I had help with the editing, but mainly from friends and my agent. Also, my wife is a writer and we always give each other feedback. As for proofreading, this is something I would recommend. I didn't use a proofreader. Several people read the manuscript to help me pick up typos but there are still a few left.

 Employ a proofreader

Proofreading is harder than it sounds! If at all possible, get someone with some professional experience to proofread your work before you publish.

WHAT WERE THE MOST CHALLENGING THINGS ABOUT THE SELF-PUBLISHING PROCESS?

I should have been much more active on blogs, Facebook and Twitter but I only did the basics. I started tweeting after the

Guardian workshop, but I'm not sure to what extent it has had an impact on book sales. Whenever there's a sudden surge of sales I try to see if it's anything to do with a tweet pattern, but I can't say I've discovered a magic solution.

The most challenging part will always be the writing. If you write a good book, the readers will come.

Attend a course

If you are serious about self-publishing, it might be worth attending a short course or workshop. Find out as much about the people running it as possible first, and try to get independent recommendations. Speaking to experts face to face can be a great help, whether you have some publishing experience already or are a newcomer.

WHAT DID YOU LEARN FROM SELF-PUBLISHING?

That you can do it yourself, be just as successful and earn more in the process without all the hassle of negotiating and being rejected.

Without self-publishing my book would still have been in the drawer. Now it has earned me £10,000 in nine months and given me a sense of empowerment. More than 22,000 people have downloaded the book. So it has done better than most traditionally published books.

IS THERE ANYTHING YOU WOULD DO DIFFERENTLY NEXT TIME?

I'd take a bit more time before publishing, but at that point I just wanted to get it out, so hindsight doesn't really mean much. It was the right thing at the time. Maybe I would work on hard copies and do some book signings in bookshops. Not that it would necessarily boost sales but I think it's nice to have a real-life anchoring. But if I do hard copies I want them to offer something extra, a tactile and visual dimension a Kindle book can't offer.

HOW DID YOU APPROACH MARKETING AND SELLING YOUR BOOKS?

I used KDP Select, mailings to friends and contacts. I was also fortunate that my book tapped into an established genre – the Scandinavian thriller.

DO YOU HAVE A WEBSITE?

Yes, but I took most of the pages down when I self-published, as they were CV-like and focused on selling myself as a screenwriting/writing tutor. Instead, I just pasted some reviews and added a contact page, which has meant that I've received a lot of comments from people who liked the book.

 Invite comments

Make sure you invite people who visit your website to comment on your book. Make it easy for them and reply to them when they do.

DO YOU USE SOCIAL MEDIA?

Twitter has sucked up a lot of my time, but it also allows direct feedback. Not sure if Amazon reviews count as social media but the immediate feedback there and through e-mail (via my website) and Twitter has been great. Of course, you get a lot of bad reviews but the good ones make up for it. It has also taught me a lot about pitching, price, etc. Readers react to price (too cheap, too expensive, impossible to get it right), references (if you compare your book to a hit book they'll tell you it isn't the same). These are all aspects I'm taking into account when writing my second book. The reviews have definitely influenced the way I approach the second book.

 Give Oliver a tweet!

Find Olivier's book *The Ice Cage* on Amazon and look at the comments to see what he might have learned from them. If the book appeals to you, buy it and leave your own comment behind. You might also like to tweet him @icecageolivier.

DID YOU HAVE ANY EXPECTATIONS FOR SALES, AND HAVE YOU MET THEM?

I didn't really have any expectations. I thought maybe a couple of thousand in the first year. That turned out to be very pessimistic, as when I put *The Ice Cage* on free for a weekend in September 2012 it reached number one in free Kindle books, which set it on a roll. After that the initial target was met within the next couple of weeks.

ARE YOU PLANNING TO SELF-PUBLISH AGAIN?

I'd love to work with an editor or publisher as teamwork is always going to benefit the book, but it would have to be a good offer, because as things stand a traditional publisher would have to offer double my current sales figures to match the income of self-publishing. It might be a better idea for me to develop as a publisher – but the problem is that when you're doing everything it leaves less time to write.

WHAT ADVICE WOULD YOU GIVE TO ANYONE ELSE PLANNING TO SELF-PUBLISH?

It's much more positive and empowering than anything you will encounter in the traditional publishing industry. Maybe it will change but there's a real pioneer spirit if you attend events organized by Byte the Book at The Ivy, or just follow self-publishing discussion online.

However, beware of self-publishing companies grabbing half of your revenues to make a cover. Fill in some metatags and upload your e-book on Amazon. Formatting is much easier than people think.

What's also clear is that even authors published by traditional publishers are required to do the same social media marketing work as self-publishers. Before going with a publisher, I recommend having a good look at what they do to give their authors and titles exposure. It doesn't take long and certainly reinforced my decision to self-publish. How many hours a day is a publisher going to spend on your book? How much will you pay the publisher (percentage of royalties)? Publishing is changing and maybe it's already becoming a sustainable model, but from what I've seen in the last year there's no way a publisher can give a small writer what self-publishing can give when it comes to value for money. And empowerment – positive as opposed to negative energy.

Self-publishing is about the book; publishing is about maintaining an industry. I'm just trying to make a living as a writer, so I know where I stand. Of course, this is a generalization and hopefully there will be more flexible publishers realizing that we need to put the story and the writer first, not the industry. Writers produce US TV series; maybe a similar model needs to be applied to publishing. Fundamentally, it's about people sharing stories and that's what we should be focusing on – nothing else. But of course I'll always be open to offers I can't refuse.

Where to next?

In Chapter 9 we look at how you can market your book effectively.

9

Marketing your book

Tom Green

For many writers the business of marketing their book is the hardest part of self-publishing. However painful it has been researching and writing the text, however much they have had to learn about editing and proofreading and formatting a manuscript, none of it seems as daunting as telling the world that the book is now on sale, and persuading people to buy it.

This is often due, in part, to the insecurity that often comes with a creative endeavour. For writers without a track record it can be very intimidating putting work on sale for the first time. And even established writers are often unsure about their latest book and would prefer it to speak for itself rather than having to promote it.

However, for all publishing, marketing is crucial. There's no need to think of it as a cynical process or something that will make you feel uncomfortable. It's about giving your book the best possible chance to reach an audience.

Why marketing matters

If you write and publish a book to communicate with other people, then the actual writing is only the first part of the process. There's no point publishing something that no one reads.

Equally, there's little point thinking that a readership will somehow find the book themselves once you have listed it on Amazon. There are hundreds of thousands of books and e-books published in the UK each year – you would have to be incredibly lucky for many people to stumble over yours unless you do something to draw it to their attention.

This doesn't mean that you must aim for record-breaking sales that shoot you to the top of the bestsellers. You can find remarkable self-publishing sales success stories online, but these are the tiny minority. Most self-published authors without a track record should be aiming for sales in the hundreds rather than the thousands. Nothing says you can't exceed this, and you shouldn't limit your ambition, but as a self-publisher it makes sense to be realistic and build step by step.

If you aim too high, there is a danger that you will feel deflated when you don't reach the targets you set. Also, you might be tempted to splash out too much on consultants in the hope that a sales boost will cover the cost.

So be realistic. Marketing is a huge area covering advertising, social media, press, film, reviews, word of mouth, pricing strategies and much more. Make a plan that you will be able to deliver and learn as much as you can as you go. Remember that every lesson learned can be applied when it comes to marketing your next book.

 What matters most...

What matters most of all is the content of your book. The better your book, the more work your readers will do for you: making recommendations in reviews, on social media and through word of mouth.

Research sales

Log on to self-publishing forums online and see if you can find out how many copies books similar to yours have sold. If no one has spoken about their sales figures, politely ask if anyone is willing to share – either on the forum or privately via e-mail. The more information you can find, the more realistic you can be about your own sales. If you find self-published books similar to yours with high sales, see what you can find out about how they were marketed.

A marketing plan

The amount of detail you put into a marketing plan ahead of publication will probably depend on how experienced you are. If you've never marketed a book or anything else before, then it's best to keep things simple and learn as you go. But even a simple plan will be useful, helping you to plan what marketing activity you can undertake and reminding you of what needs to be done in the midst of the excitement of getting the book ready for sale.

HOW MUCH TIME DO YOU HAVE?

If you are working full-time and have three young children then you probably feel that you simply don't have time to devote to marketing your book. However, if you have found enough time to write it, then you should be able to find time to help sell it. Remember, that's at least part of the point of publishing. Most self-publishers find themselves stretched for time, since most are doing it in addition to other work or responsibilities. You should, of course, be realistic about how many hours a week you can devote to marketing, but don't use your busy schedule as an excuse for not getting stuck into the business of promoting your book. If you really don't have time, but do have some money, then consider contracting out marketing to a consultant. (See the end of this chapter for more on this.)

Fit marketing into your schedule

Sketch out a timetable of your week. Where could you find time for marketing? Once your book is finished, could you use what was once writing time as marketing time?

Countdown to the launch

In publishing, the launch of a book really counts. That's not to say that your marketing should stop once the book is out, or that you shouldn't try to build an audience over time – you should. But the launch is an event that media and readers can latch on to. Pick a date that will give you the best possible opportunity to get attention for your work, and when you will have some spare time to handle enquiries. Certain times of year might suit certain types of book – for example, diet and exercise books normally come out in the New Year when people have made fitness resolutions. But sometimes avoiding those popular times can give your book more chance to stand out.

Once you have picked a date, count backwards and plan your marketing activity week by week. If you haven't left yourself enough time, either consider pushing back the launch date or, if that's not possible, see if you can concentrate your marketing into that timeframe.

Remember, the launch date doesn't need to be when the book is actually published. In fact, it's better to wait for at least a few weeks after that (perhaps more) to allow time to check for problems, send out review copies and get your other marketing activity done.

If possible, try to organize some kind of launch event that will appeal to your target audience and provide an opportunity to sell books. People will expect you to do a short reading from your new work and to talk a little about it… and to have a drink or two. Think carefully about what budget you have for the event and whether the prospective sales make the spending worth while. It can be difficult to judge, but make sure you don't spend more money than you can afford to lose.

Make sure you invite media contacts to the launch and use social media to generate interest. Arrange for someone else to take photographs and then share them online afterwards. It's all about creating a 'buzz' – the sense that your book is being read and talked about.

The launch is crucial

The launch of your book is likely to be your best opportunity for marketing. People are attracted to something new, and you should do everything possible to generate interest in the launch and be prepared to deal with enquiries, comments and purchases.

Target audience

Some writers will have a target audience in mind right from their book's conception. For others, a book is entirely personal and they give no thought to whom it might appeal to.

When it comes to marketing, however, identifying the target audience is key. Once you know who they are, you can work out how to reach them.

Your target audience is likely to be people who have bought similar books in the past or have an interest in the subject you are writing about. You will find them in online forums, on social media and through specialist publications and websites.

In some ways it is helpful if your book has the potential to appeal to a very wide audience. An historical novel, for example, could be read by hundreds of thousands of people. But this also presents a difficulty. It takes huge amounts of money, contacts and expertise to target a broad audience, and even then a book is often lost in the crowd.

It's far easier to target smaller groups of people with specialist interests. That might be obvious if your book is non-fiction. But even with fiction try to narrow things down – perhaps there is a genre, theme or a setting or character that might appeal to a certain audience you can target.

Narrowing down the audience for your marketing doesn't mean that the book won't have a chance to appeal more broadly. In the end, the book's content will determine how widely read it is. But the more that you can focus your marketing effort at the outset, the more likely you are to get some momentum and begin on the road to selling hundreds of copies rather than just a few dozen.

Endorsements

Even established authors frequently seek endorsements for a book from fellow authors or experts in the relevant field to help promote their book when it is launched. If you don't have a track record then you will find it difficult to get well-known people to read your work, let alone recommend it, but that doesn't mean you shouldn't try.

More realistically, try to think of someone to read and endorse it who would appeal to your target audience.

For example, is there another self-published author in the same genre with a good sales record whom you could approach? Even if they are only known to a few thousand people, those people will be part of your key target audience.

Another idea is to approach well-respected local writers or booksellers. They might be more willing to read your work and their endorsement will mean something to people in your area.

Social media and blogging

One of the main drivers behind the rise of self-publishing has been the spread of social media like Twitter and Facebook. Mainstream publishers used to have a massive advantage because of their access to the printed media and radio; it was very difficult to get any coverage without having some kind of personal contact. Now, even the biggest publishers find social media a significant marketing tool. Authors, whether first-timers or Man Booker Prize-winners, are expected to be active tweeters and, though there are a few who still opt out, most realize that social media are an invaluable tool for promoting their work.

It would be a mistake, however, to see social media purely as a marketing tool. It can be used that way – making posts about your upcoming work, book deals and positive reviews – but Twitter and Facebook are most effective when they are used genuinely socially. That means reading and responding to other people's posts, interacting whenever possible, and posting about a wider range of topics than just your work.

Think before you post

Laws of libel and copyright still apply on Twitter and Facebook, and even if you delete a post someone might already have saved it (and it will be saved on the host company's server). So, while informality and strong opinions are normally welcomed, you should still think before you post.

TWITTER

A Twitter profile, which is free to sign up for, is like having a web page on which you can make short 'posts' of no more than 140 characters. Unless you protect your profile (which, as an author seeking publicity, you are unlikely to do), it can, in theory, be seen on the Web by anyone anywhere in the world.

In practice, it will usually only be seen by people who choose to 'follow' you. You see every post made by someone you follow – and you can follow as many people as you like. Unless they 'protect' their tweets, you can follow anyone you like – but remember that other people can see who you follow and who follows you.

When you first join Twitter it can feel overwhelming. There are millions of Twitter profiles from all over the world and some people seem to make a new post several times a minute. The best approach is a gradual one. Use the Twitter search box to find some people you know you would like to follow – perhaps well-known authors, or publishers, journalists, friends or family – and get used to how it all works. You don't have to post at all until you're ready, but people will probably only start following you when you do.

If you put someone's Twitter name in a tweet – for example @stephenfry – they will be notified in the 'connections' part of their account. Very famous people are unlikely to respond due to the sheer volume of tweets they get, but with the less celebrated it can be a good way to connect. You might want to tell an author how much you enjoyed their book, or a theatre how much you liked a play.

Normally after a few weeks people start to find Twitter addictive. Once you are following more than a few hundred people – and Twitter makes continual suggestions about whom you might follow, based on whom you follow so far – you'll find that rather than trying to read every tweet that comes your way, you need to dip in and out.

There are lots of ways to manage your Twitter use, using lists and apps for your phone or PC. Once you've mastered the basics, start researching online if you have any problems or difficulties.

From a marketing point of view Twitter has two main functions.

The first is as a kind of broadcaster to your followers so that you can tell them about your book. Unless you are already well known, it will probably take many months to build up more than a few hundred followers, so time spent on Twitter is a long-term investment. But these followers are likely to be your prime audience; people who have shown an interest in you and might be interested in buying your book. Don't bombard them with self-promotion, but don't be shy of letting your Twitter followers know about your book launch. They are then likely to be your first target for ongoing promotions such as discounts and giveaways.

The second use of Twitter is for making new contacts. As mentioned above, you can tweet anyone. They might not respond but, if you can identify them as part of your target audience, then it's worth a go.

FACEBOOK

A normal Facebook profile shares many similarities with Twitter. It's about connecting, interacting, commenting and sharing. Facebook has always been more about 'friends', however genuine, and online conversation but you can still use it to help market your books.

The biggest difference from Twitter is that you can only be someone's 'friend' – the equivalent of following them on Twitter – if they give permission. On the plus side that means that connections can be more genuine, but it also means that it can be hard to build up connections with people outside those you already know.

For your book you could create a separate Facebook Page – these are used by organizations and companies and can be 'Liked' by anyone, without permission. Creating a Page can help separate your personal life from your publishing life, but it's also an extra element to maintain.

Facebook can certainly be a fantastic marketing tool, especially if you have events to publicize and pictures and videos to share. But if you're not already a regular Facebook user then for marketing purposes you are probably better off sticking to Twitter.

BLOGGING

Blogs – simple websites in a diary format with the newest post at the top of the page – have been somewhat overshadowed by the rise of social media. But they remain a key tool for the self-publisher, and one that can interact with your other marketing devices.

If your main website keeps most of the same content from month to month (information about you and your work), and your social media changes every day or even every hour, a blog can fit somewhere in between. You might make a new post every week or so, perhaps a reflection on something you have been writing about or something you have read.

The tone is often informal, and blog posts can be any length you choose, but they are a chance to publish at greater length than the 140 characters of a tweet.

From a marketing point of view, blogs are a shop window into your writing and you as a person. If you can engage an audience, they will be much more likely to buy your book, even if your blog posts are not directly related to it.

If you are good at writing short blog posts and articles, you should also enquire about contributing to other magazines and blogs. Many of them won't be able to pay you for articles, but if you have something interesting to say they might be willing to provide you with a platform.

As with all marketing activity, don't spend more time on this than you can afford!

Don't get bogged down in blogs!

Time spent on social media and blogging can be time well spent. But don't forget that the main thing writers need to do is write!

Reviews

Unless you are an established author, you are unlikely to get reviews in the mainstream press. If appropriate, you should send review copies to specialist and local press, once you have made contact to establish who would be the best person to send it to. But in the main you will rely on reviews by readers.

Reader reviews have been the cause of much controversy in recent years. With so many sites, most notably Amazon, using prominent rating systems, authors have tried many ways of influencing them in order to promote sales.

The simple truth is that reviews, especially on Amazon, really can make a difference, but it's a mistake to try to trick the system. For example, creating fake profiles to post positive reviews will, if discovered, seriously undermine your credibility – it is known as 'sock-puppeting' and amounts to committing fraud. Of course, you can invite friends to post reviews in the hope they will be positive, but on the whole you just have to accept whatever gets posted.

It can be worth while sending out free review copies in the hope that people will read the book, like it, and post positive reviews in time for the book's launch. This has certainly worked for some established self-publishers with a strong following, but it might be less easy to orchestrate if you don't yet have a track record and a readership.

Another approach is to try specialist self-publishing sites. A good list can be found in this article and in the comments beneath it: www.guardian.co.uk/books/booksblog/2012/nov/19/self-published-books-where-to-find.

 ## Get into the reviewing habit

Get into the habit of reviewing books yourself for online communities and retail sites. If you make a real effort to be fair, and to understand the author's intentions, it can be a great way to get yourself thinking more deeply about what you read. It will also introduce you to the huge community of online reader reviewers and you might be able to make some useful contacts who will review your own work.

Price-cuts and giveaways

As self-publishing e-books has grown in popularity there has been a general acceptance among authors that free giveaways are a vital part of building an audience. The idea is that by giving away one book for free, you generate interest and reader reviews.

If you have published other books, then it might also make people more likely to buy one.

For e-books this is possible (if the retailer / self-publishing company allows it) because there are no production costs. With printed books you're unlikely to be able to afford to give many away for free, but you could consider offering discounts.

Amazon, the largest retail platform for e-books, has changed the way it governs pricing and at the moment you can normally give books away for free only if you join the Kindle Direct Publishing scheme. See the chapter on e-books for more information about how the different self-publishing platforms approach pricing.

If you are going to give discounts of any kind, it's best to make them time limited and to promote them as much as you can without annoying people! You might start with a reduced price to generate interest, then go to the standard price and then return to a discount when the initial interest has flagged.

Stick to your pricing plan

Have a plan for pricing your book and stick to it. Don't chop and change every few days just to try to generate interest or it will seem unprofessional.

How to commission marketing support

There are lots of companies and consultants advertising marketing support, and some self-publishing companies offer it as part of a package.

As with any commissioning, establish very clearly what you will get before you sign up. Shop around to compare prices and services and ask to have contact with people they have worked for already.

Don't be blinded by jargon that might sound more impressive than it actually is. And, when it comes to the bottom line, try to estimate how many sales the money you will spend might deliver. If possible, ask other authors who have commissioned similar services how it has worked out for them.

Review your progress

Whether you are a marketing veteran or a complete novice, make time to review your progress at regular intervals.

It can help to do this with someone else, explaining what you've done so far, what you hoped to achieve and how the results have panned out. Even if they lack expertise, they might have a different perspective that proves useful, and sometimes just having to explain something can make it clearer for you.

Another way to do this is online. If you can connect with other self-publishers online, it can be really helpful to post updates and self-assessments of your progress and then to ask questions. A blog can be a good place for this, and if you are happy to share your experiences, you will probably find that other authors are interested to see how your approach has fared.

Although in some sense self-publishers are in competition, in practice you will find that many people are happy to co-operate and help one another to improve.

You should also make time to read up on the subject of marketing; like all aspects of writing and self-publishing, there are always possibilities for improvement. There are lots of interesting articles you can find online, but two authors you could start with are Tim Ferriss and Seth Godin. Both are American, and both have had huge success as self-publishers. Don't feel you have to try to emulate them, or follow their methods, but both have interesting insights into marketing and self-publishing.

Focus points

- Don't be shy about marketing. The point of publishing is to get people to read your book.
- Draw up a simple marketing plan before you start.
- Make the most of your launch, even if you don't have money for a launch event.
- Get active on social media as soon as possible. The more you put into them, the more benefit you will gain.
- Use price discounts and giveaways, but don't chop and change your price so much that you confuse people.

Where to next?

In Chapter 10 we look at how you can set up and run an author's website – another crucial way in which you can promote your work.

10

Setting up and running a website

Tom Green

While at one time setting up a website was expensive and running it required specialist knowledge and training, it can now be done for free.

A number of online tools exist that aim to enable non-experts to create professional-looking websites. There are also numerous paid-for services both online and via companies and individual consultants. If you are thinking of paying to help set up your site, make sure you check out the free sites first to make sure any expense incurred is necessary.

Do you need a website?

There are various places you can create web pages without having to set up a whole site. They include Amazon Author Pages, Lulu Storefront and other pages provided by self-publishing services or retailers.

It is certainly worth making use of these pages, and, if you have limited time or expertise, you might decide that one or more of these is sufficient. They will provide a place online for people to find information about you and a link you can give for people to see your books. They are free, easy to use and, in most cases, easy to update.

However, your own website allows you to impose your own personality online and to create the environment that best suits your books. You will have more flexibility in terms of design, content and additional 'plug-in' content like YouTube videos and Twitter feeds.

A website can establish your identity as an author, becoming the single authoritative place where readers, potential readers, media and retailers can find information about you and your work.

Assess some authors' websites

Do a web search on some of your favourite authors including self-published authors working in the same genre as you. Can you find their websites? What features do they have? Do you think they promote the author's work effectively?

How to set up a free website

Popular free website-building services include Moonfruit, Weebly and Wix. A web search will also reveal several others. If you are looking for a free service, check the terms and conditions carefully before you commit yourself. For example, some sites charge for hosting – that is, for providing an online space for your site.

The aim of these services is to make it easy for people with little or no web expertise to set up a site.

All you need to do is sign up with your e-mail address and you will be able to select from set designs into which you can put your own images and content. You will be able to modify the design elements to varying extents, depending on your technical proficiency and the flexibility of the various services. For example, Weebly allows full editing access to the style sheets containing the code that creates the page.

One of the great things about these services is that it is very easy just to sign up and have a go. Although once you publish the site it will be online for all to see, it's very unlikely that anyone will find it at first unless you send them the link because it normally takes search engines several weeks to index new sites. So you can play around, experiment with different layouts and designs and try the different tools. You can also get feedback, both in person and by sharing the link via social media.

How to get the right domain name

Many of the free sites make their money by selling you a domain name. Typically, they will offer you a free one that involves their domain name, for example janesmithauthor.weebly.com.

There is nothing wrong with those free domains, but if you want something similar such as janesmithauthor.co.uk then you will have to pay for it.

Only one person can own a domain name at any one time, so if someone has beaten you to it then you will just have to wait until it becomes available. If your first choice – normally involving your name or the title of your book – for either a free or paid-for domain is not available, then think creatively for a version of the name. Try to keep it short and, as far as possible, ensure that it makes sense to someone seeing it for the first time.

Buying a domain name

Free website-building sites normally offer an easy way to get your domain name – you buy it through them and they automatically assign it to the website you build with them. However, while this is the most convenient way to get a domain name, you will probably find it cheaper to buy it elsewhere from one of the many domain registration services such as www.123reg.co.uk. They have easy-to-follow instructions and prices are normally low for .co.uk domains. But you will need to work out how to connect your site to this new domain.

The service you use for your free site should explain how to transfer it to an external domain, but the terminology can vary so you might need to get help from a friend with some web experience or else by asking via social media or on one of the many forums dedicated to the popular web-building tools.

Research a domain name

Go to www.123.reg.co.uk and use their search tool to find out which domain names relating to your name or the title of your book are available, and how much they cost.

Domain names ending in .com are normally more expensive than those ending .co.uk. Unless you have realistic aspirations to sell internationally, you should probably stick to .co.uk (.org domains are for organizations).

Simple tips for website design

When designing your own website it makes sense to follow one of the templates that is provided. Unless you have real skills in design, and can make something unusual and striking, the key is to organize content on the page in a way that is easy to read at a glance.

People tend to browse on the Internet, flitting from site to site, so you have only a few seconds to make it clear who you are, the title of your book, what it is about and why they should buy it.

That doesn't mean that you need to SHOUT IN CAPITAL LETTERS and use lots of exclamation marks!!! Nor should you splash colour and moving text all over your site. And under no circumstances have music playing automatically when people arrive.

All of those things are likely to annoy people and make them leave your site straight away.

Think carefully about the most important information you want to provide and organize it on the page in a clear way that suits the tone and genre of your book. Use appropriate colours and images and always get copyright clearance for any images you use.

 Match your website with your book

> Your website is a tool for selling your book and so should embody the qualities, genre and tone of that book. Make it easy for people browsing the Web to understand what your book is about and why they should buy it. Think about colours, fonts and overall style for your site in the same way that you do for the cover of your book.

Try not to put too much content on each page. Even people interested in your work probably won't scroll far down on their screen, and some might be using small laptops, so keep the most important information high up.

Don't be afraid of white space. Lots of very professional websites use lots of white space to help the rest of the content stand out and to give the impression of a calm and measured design.

Assess 'first impressions'

Search for the websites of five authors working in the same genre as you. If possible, find a mix of corporately published and self-published. Consider your first impressions of the sites. Before you even read the words, what impressions do the sites create? Does the tone and feel of the site tell you much about the author's work?

Now think about the tone and feel of your own work and consider what elements on your website will help convey that. For example, what colours will you choose, what images and what style of font?

138

The importance of 'usability'

'Usability', as you might guess, refers to how easy a website is to use. As mentioned above, a great-looking website is not the first priority – it's no good at all unless people browsing the Internet can find what they want from your site.

As well as clear and well-organized design, usability is also improved by the language you use, the structure you give your site and how you use links.

LANGUAGE

The general rule for websites is to say what you mean, especially with headings and titles. While newspapers and magazines often use clever titles with puns and intriguing language, when reading online people are not normally willing to invest the time to find out what you mean. They want to scan the page and understand whether it is worth their while reading on.

Of course, you might want to challenge this conventional wisdom, especially if your book is unconventional. But if not, use clear simple language. Try to use as few words as possible, but if you need to use an extra word to make things clear, then use it.

Because people tend to scan web pages at speed, headings and subheadings are particularly important. They give the website user something to focus on. So do images, as long as they relate closely to the content of the text.

STRUCTURE

For a website relating to a book, or even a series of books, the structure of your site is unlikely to be complex. We'll discuss some of the key content for your site later in the chapter, but whatever you include, make sure it is easy for the first-time visitor to your site to see clearly where everything is. If there are processes for them to go through – for example, to contact you or to buy your book – these should be clear and intuitive.

LINKS

You should use links in moderation, but they can be very helpful. From your homepage, you should link through to key content on your site. For example, you should have at least one link that takes people straight to somewhere they can buy your book. You will probably also want a link that takes them to more information about the book. There will already be links in the 'navigation' at the top or by the side of the page, but it's still a good idea to make these important links prominent elsewhere on the homepage.

You should also offer links to other sites, where appropriate. If there are positive reviews of your book, then you should both quote from them and link to them. If there is a good reason – for example if they are relevant to the research or background of your book – provide some links to external sources; they will help establish the credibility of your work.

Any web-building tool will show you how to make web links and will automatically make them stand out in bold, a different colour, or underlined, or some combination of those three. It's important that visitors to your site can identify links quickly, so don't make any text that isn't a link either bold, a different colour or underlined.

Key content on an author's website

Most good authors' websites have much the same kind of content. You will certainly need the following features:

HOMEPAGE

This is the 'front cover' of your website. It should give a clear and appealing impression of your work and should contain links to key content within the site, especially to where people can buy the book.

YOUR BOOK TITLE

If you have published several books, you can give each their own section or put them all under one heading. Give a concise summary of the contents, along with recommendations, positive reviews and links to where the book can be bought. Underneath this you might like to add something longer about the background to the book and how you came to write it.

ABOUT ME

Whether you have had an ordinary life or an extraordinary one, readers tend to want to know something about you. If biographical details are relevant to the book, then you can go into some detail. And, if your life story is remarkable in some way, don't be shy – let the world know!

CONTACT ME

If you put an e-mail address on a website, it will attract spam, but it is important that people can get in touch if they need to. Many e-mail clients these days are good at filtering out spam, so it need not be a problem. If your e-mail address gets clogged up with spam, consider creating an e-mail with another free provider such as Google's gmail.com which has a good spam filter.

PRESS AND REVIEWS

Here you can list positive feedback. Don't quote reviews or comments at length unless there are no web links for them.

NEWS

If you have news to report on a reasonably regular basis – about once a month – then you can create a news section for updates about any book signings or promotional activity.

TWITTER AND FACEBOOK

If you have social media accounts, you should be able to embed them in your website. That means your status updates and tweets can appear automatically in a box on your site. It's a good way to connect your different online activities. Follow the instructions from Twitter and Facebook about how to do this, and also look in the 'Help' section of the website-building service you are using.

Your website is your hub

Your website should be a central place connecting all of your online activity. Make it easy for people to find what they want.

How to use a blog

In addition to the content above, you might also choose to create a blog. Most free website tools offer a blog that can be a part of your website, so it should be easy to set up.

Blogs allow you to upload content – text, photos or video, or some combination of the three – that is automatically dated and archived. This means the newest content you upload is always at the top of the page. Older content gets pushed down the page and neatly stored.

Blogs are often written in quite a personal way, emphasizing the author's opinions and experiences. But you can write yours in any way you choose. However, if you are writing your blog on a site whose main purpose is to promote your book then you might want to restrict your blog content to something related to that book, or to your experiences as a self-publishing author.

Assess some authors' blogs

Type 'author's blogs' into your search engine and read a selection of the sites you find. Note down which ones appeal to you and why. Are the posts always directly related to the author's own book?

Connecting your website with social media

One benefit of writing a blog is that it gives you fresh content to promote via social media. You can't keep repeating posts on Twitter and Facebook promoting your book – people will soon get bored and annoyed – but you can post about new items on your blog. You will need to invest time and effort in writing the new content, but it's a great way of showing people how you think and getting them to your website from where, hopefully, they will buy your book.

As mentioned above, you can also 'embed' your tweets and Facebook updates into your site. They won't always make sense out of context, but they will add freshness to your website (as long as your social media content is updated every few days) and encourage people to connect with you.

Selling books from your website

It is quite easy to sell books directly from your website. Many free and low-cost sites have 'shopping cart' functions that you can use. If you are only selling one or a few books, then this should be quite easy to set up, with payments normally made through an online system such as PayPal.

The main reason for doing this will be if you are self-publishing without support from a company that will process and fulfil orders. If you choose to do this, then it is easier than ever to manage the online sales process yourself.

The main challenge is likely to be fulfilment – that is, wrapping and despatching the books to customers. You will need to decide how much to charge and make sure you have enough time to deal with orders.

One possible drawback of selling directly from your own site is that potential customers might be wary of making payments if you have no track record. So make sure you are very clear about who you are, how they can get in touch with you if they have problems, and how the payment and fulfilment process will be carried out.

Bear in mind that people are used to prompt despatches from sites like Amazon, so might be unhappy waiting for more than a few days. You will also need to work out what to do if people say that books have not arrived or if they arrive damaged.

However, if you are familiar with a site like eBay, then none of this will be new to you.

Even if you are self-publishing independently, you might still decide that you don't want the hassle of processing orders. In that case you can simply point people towards a retail site where your book is listed.

Ways to improve your search rankings

'Search ranking' refers to how high up the page your website comes when someone searches for a certain thing. The aim is to come as high up as possible so that there is the greatest chance that someone will visit your website.

For general searches, it is unlikely that you will get much benefit from search engines. For example, if you have written a contemporary love story, there will be many thousands of search results for 'contemporary love story' from bigger sites and more established writers that will come above yours.

But with more specific searches you might fare better. If people search your name or the title of your book, then you want your site to figure prominently in the rankings. And searches might also be beneficial in relation to specific aspects of your book. For example, if it concerns a particular place or a particular issue, then there is a chance you might be able to build a good ranking if you can set your site up well and make it popular.

Setting up your site

Most website-building services will automatically prompt you to do certain things that work well with search engines. These include giving your site a title and naming individual pages. Make sure you include a clear summary of your book in text on the homepage so that search engines can pick that up as well.

CONTENT

Search engines tend to like 'natural language' content – that is, words you write that are genuine rather than attempts to repeat lots of key words in the hope that search engines will notice them. Natural language headings and subheadings are also important. Try to avoid repeating content on different pages, other than for small sections such as quotations from reviews that might appear on both the homepage and inside.

NEW CONTENT

The more new content you can add, the better. That's why blogs are good. Don't sacrifice the quality of your site for the sake of adding content but, if you can, regularly add relevant blog posts – it will definitely help your search ranking.

LINKS AND INTERACTIONS

The more you can get people to link to your site and comment on your blog, the better. Don't sign up for any link exchange programs, as search engines hate those and might even blacklist you. But if you let people know about your website and, most importantly, create interesting content that prompts them to visit and post links on their own site and on social media, then your search ranking will rise.

METADATA

On a small website, metadata – text that doesn't appear on the published site but is used to inform search engines – will not matter too much. But most website-building tools give the chance to use metadata and it is worth doing. Simply follow the instructions to add simple text describing your site and, if possible, each page.

PAID-FOR SERVICES

There are lots of companies that offer to improve your search ranking. Some will do a good job, but proceed with caution – if you follow the instructions above you will have done most of what is possible. If you do commission someone to do this work, ask them to be explicit about what they will do and remember to be wary of any tricks such as 'link farms' or 'link exchanges' that might improve your ranking in the short term but could end up getting you blacklisted from search engines.

Try this

Do an Internet search on a subject relating to your book. Which sites come top? Is there any way you could persuade them to feature or promote your work?

Google Analytics

Google Analytics is a free tool that enables you to monitor how many people come to which parts of your website, which sites they were referred from, which search terms were used and many other things besides.

It's normally relatively simple to install. Just check the help section of the website-building tool you are using. It can seem complicated to use at first, but it can be interesting to see how people are finding your site and which bits they are reading.

If you are running a well-planned marketing campaign, then it allows you to see which parts of it are proving most effective at bringing people to your site.

Setting up web pages on other websites

Whether you set up your own site or not, you should also set up a free page on any other retail or listing site where it is available. If you are offered the chance for a paid-for page, be careful before you commit and check with others who have used the service to see whether it is worth while.

The templates for free pages will be more restrictive than your own website, but your approach should be similar. Communicate clearly and concisely in a style and tone that reflects the content of your book and acts as a strong advertisement for it.

Commissioning a website

If you can afford it, there are many individuals and companies whom you can commission to build a website for you. The following is useful advice:

- As with all services you commission, shop around and try to get personal recommendations either from people you know or other authors you connect with online.
- Ask different companies or consultants to submit a proposal and a budget as well as references and links to sites they have previously built.
- Be clear about what you want. Do you just need some help with design? Do you need someone to help you through the whole process? Will you be able to update the site yourself, or do you need to pay someone to do it?
- If you are going to do the updates yourself, ask to try out the editing system that will be used – there are many different ones – so that you know you will be able to do it.

- Be sure to ask about the costs of hosting and make sure you have access to the site where your site's domain name is registered. If, for some reason, you lose contact with the person who built the site you still want to be able to access the domain name.
- Also be clear about any ongoing costs for updates or maintenance, and be clear what these will entail. Try to ensure that you will be able to take the website to another company in the future if you choose to do so and are not locked in with the company that built the site, even if their prices rise.

Focus points

- Experiment with a free website tool. You might find it easier than you think.
- Keep the content and design for your website clear and concise.
- Have prominent links to the most important content.
- If you can find the time, create a blog and write new posts at least once a month.
- Connect your social media and blog with your website.

Where to next?

In Chapter 11 we will look at what happens after your book is published.

11

Post-publication

Kevin McCann

Well, it's decision time again and the question is: what next? Do you want to carry on writing and, if you do, do you want to continue developing your skills as a writer?

If the answer to these questions is yes, read on.

If the answer's no, read on anyway. You might change your mind.

In his poem 'Flying Crooked', Robert Graves compares the flight of a butterfly – by implication – to the mind of a poet. He was not the first writer, nor will he be the last, to point out that creative thinking and logical thinking are, apparently, two entirely different things. This has led to the idea that creative people are impractical, illogical, exotic beings who can't think straight. And, contrariwise, that logical people can only think in straight lines, are good at things like maths but are hopelessly dull company.

This led to the notion that there were two types of thinking, and in the 1950s the psychologist J.P. Guilford coined the terms 'convergent' and 'divergent' to differentiate between them.

Convergent thinking: thinking that brings together information focused on solving a problem, especially solving problems that have a single correct solution. A good example of this would be a maths problem for which there is only one correct answer.

For example: In a group of four people, A weighs 120 pounds; B weighs 140 pounds; C weighs 200 pounds and D weighs 130 pounds. What is the average weight of the group?

The correct answer, if you care at all, is 147.5 pounds, and to get the right answer you need to follow a logical sequence – that is, add the four weights together and then divide by four.

There is a set method and only one correct solution.

Divergent thinking: thinking in an unusual and un-stereotyped way to generate several possible solutions to a problem. Or, thinking that moves away in diverging directions so as to involve a variety of aspects which sometimes lead to novel ideas and solutions; often associated with creativity.

Divergent thinking is also known as lateral thinking, a term coined by Edward De Bono in 1967.

This apparent split has led many people into a kind of either/or mentality – that is, you're either one kind of thinker or another. Ask any experienced teacher and they'll tell you that's nonsense. In reality, we're all a mixture of the two and most of us can switch between types of thinking depending on the task in hand.

If you're writing a poem, you tend to think divergently, but not always. Your poem has to have what I call a poetic logic so that your reader may not be able to explain the poem's literal meaning, but they can still understand it emotionally. The line 'Macbeth hath murdered sleep' is a logical impossibility – how can you kill sleep? – but anyone who's ever had a sleepless night brought on by stress knows exactly what it means.

Even cartoons have an internal logic – characters run off cliffs but never fall *until* they've looked down.

If you have a series of maths problems to solve, you'll probably think convergently; on the other hand, if you're launching a new business or book, you may follow all the tried-and-tested marketing strategies… and then come up with something new that nobody, as far as you know, has tried before.

As a self-published (and therefore self-promoting) writer you need to be convergent or divergent depending on circumstances.

 ## Albert Einstein, theoretical physicist

'Creativity is the residue of time wasted.'

I suspect Einstein was being heavily ironic in the same way Oscar Wilde was when he claimed that 'All art is quite useless.' It all depends how you define your terms.

Anyway, let's get back to time wasted – for me, time wasted is when I expend a lot of energy on something that isn't of the slightest importance and, in the end, just wears me out.

Time not wasted is time spent enriching my life. So time wasted could be, for example, writing sarcastic comments on Facebook about some politician or other. It's often – no, scrub that – it's always an excuse not to start writing.

Time spent usefully could be reading, walking, writing letters, listening to music, baking a cake… the list goes on and on.
The point is this: deep down, you know the difference between meditation and procrastination. You know it the way a small child trying to postpone bedtime knows it.

Prioritizing and time management

If you're serious about building a career for yourself as a writer, you need to start organizing your time around your writing. How much or how little time you've got available obviously depends on your personal circumstances.

If you've got a job and/or family commitments, finding the time and energy to write as well is very difficult. And as I've already mentioned, the 'heroic exhaustion leads to glorious visions' myth is just that: a myth, and a dangerous one at that.

We all need balance in our lives so what you need to do is sit down and draw up a schedule for yourself that's realistic. And don't worry. There are lots of ways you can use your downtime to help your writing.

SLEEP ON IT

For as long I've been writing, I've had the habit of rereading the last page I wrote that day just before going to bed. I've often found that when I go back to it the next day, I get much more written than if I simply 'forget it' until my next writing session. My own theory is that, while I'm sleeping, the part of my brain where my dreams come from is active – I dream a lot; meanwhile, my conscious mind has all but completely closed down. But not completely; one small part of it spends the night mulling things over.

HAVE A FEW LAUGHS

I found that when I was working on a particular piece and was feeling either completely blocked, too stressed to cope or just generally riddled with self-doubt and whining self-pity, that a few laughs really helped.

I began to realize that it wasn't just the rush of energizing endorphins that helped; it was also the divergent thinking found in really great comedy, whether it's visual like Keaton or Chaplin, or verbal like Tommy Cooper or Groucho Marx, or both. Humour often describes a world in which the laws of logic don't apply. It's a world we all need to visit from time to time, not just because it does you good physically but because it aids your creative faculty. In humour the only limit is your own inventiveness.

It's something that is being rediscovered by psychologists but has been known by supposedly primitive people for ever. Hence the tradition of the sacred clown because:

 Black Elk, Lakota shaman

'Laughing or crying, it's still the same face.'

DO SOME HOUSEWORK

Again, my own experience coupled with conversations with other writers has confirmed that such humble tasks as ironing, washing the dishes and peeling potatoes during your downtime enhances your work.

I think there are two reasons for this.

Firstly, your intellect as well as your body needs rest. If you never switch off, you'll end up either physically or mentally ill. A quick word of warning here. There are people who think that what they call 'madness' actually helps creativity. They're the sort who believe the 'Van Gogh blindly inspired genius' myth. Now it is true that a lot of artists – I'm using the word to cover everyone who creates, so that includes musicians, visual artists and so on as well as writers – suffer from mental illnesses of one kind or another. I think that it's also true that, in many cases, creativity helps the individual cope with the illness. It's the thread that leads out of the maze. I speak here from personal experience.

Secondly, it's good to remind yourself that being a writer does not make you better than other people nor does it absolve you from the ordinary mundane tasks. Taking your turn emptying the waste bins is not only helpful, it keeps you grounded. I've noticed that the self-appointed literary genius whose artistic temperament puts them above the rest of us is often, in reality, a terrible writer and a dreadful human being.

No surprise when you think about it: how can you write convincingly about people if you think most of them are beneath you?

GRAB SOME SOLITUDE

Everyone, whether they write or not, needs time to themselves. How little or how much time depends on individual circumstances. If you live alone, you can have all the solitude you want. If you don't, you have to adapt.

I tend to get up early and once I've fed the cat I can spend an hour daydreaming before I start work. I never open a newspaper, listen to the radio or watch breakfast TV. I find them intrusive and irritating.

I've discovered that, by doing this, I get much more written every day. I've also discovered that I write best in the morning.

FIND THE BEST TIME TO WRITE...

As I've pointed out elsewhere, there's no one-size-fits-all method when it comes to writing. Find the time that suits you best and fits in with the rest of your life and then begin to build a schedule round that.

If you have a job and/or family commitments, then sit down and work out a realistic schedule. Ideally, what you're after is a working week that includes your non-writing commitments, your downtime and regular set periods when you can work uninterrupted.

Once you've done all that, as much as possible, stick to it.

Extending your network

As well as your website, blog, Facebook and Twitter, you should also plan out a strategy for extending your local network. I'd begin with local radio and newspapers.

For local papers, start with a visit to their website. Find the name of the appropriate contact, which you will probably find listed under features or local news, and send them a brief e-mail introducing yourself, telling them you've just had a book published and asking if they're interested.

Make a note of the date and if you haven't heard anything after a week or so, resend the same e-mail and ask politely whether they've had time to consider your proposal. If you don't get a reply to that one, forget it. They're not interested.

The chances are that someone will get back to you. Local dailies have to be filled six days a week, so, if it's interesting, they'll probably want to cover it. If they do, don't expect this to be the start of regular local press coverage. It won't be. What it will be is a chance to publicize your book locally.

Local radio stations are usually happy to get as many studio guests on as they can and in my experience, are always helpful and encouraging.

Research local media

Before you contact either local radio or newspapers, do some research. Have a look at their respective websites and see if there's a specific journalist/presenter who deals with local interest/arts events and contact them directly.

Jonathan Dean, radio producer

'Essentially the book needs to be interesting and relatable to the audience. The author needs to be able to speak well in a conversational style and react to the dialogue without the need for notes – otherwise it can just sound staged – it's all about being as natural and as interesting as possible.'

If you're invited to appear on local radio, don't forget to Facebook and tweet the date and time. Do the same if you're going to be featured in the local paper.

Don't expect to be paid

You won't be, but you may gain in other ways.

My one appearance on Radio City (Liverpool) led to me being asked to write ghost stories, which were then featured on City Talk… which led to me publishing a collection… which was then promoted by Pete Price (the host on City Talk)… which led to a selection of the stories being recorded and remastered by Jonathan Dean (a producer at Radio City) and then sold as downloads… which in turn raised my profile considerably.

However, don't assume that one appearance on local radio will suddenly change everything. Most of the time, once you're finished it'll be 'Thanks very much… Here's the exit' and that will be that. It's not because media people are shallow – it's because they're busy and you're one of maybe a dozen studio guests they've looked after just that week. So don't start asking when you can be on again.

If you do have an idea that you think they might be interested in – new short stories, local history, folklore, theatre reviews and so on – get back in touch. Again, I'd suggest an e-mail.

You might also want to look at community radio as a place where you can both raise your profile and gain some valuable broadcasting experience. Go on to the Internet and find out where the nearest station is, contact them, tell them about your book and ask if they're interested. If you are interviewed, ask if you can have a copy and put it on your website as an mp3.

If you have a good 'radio voice', publicize your book every chance you get. It may lead you into more work.

LIBRARIES

If you're already a member of a readers' group, you can publicize your book there. Find out if there are other groups within a reasonable distance of where you live and see if it's possible for you to visit them as well.

If your book is print-on-demand as well as e-published, take a few copies with you to sell. By all means, offer a small discount if you can afford it but don't give them away. It makes you look desperate.

Take business cards giving your contact and website details and give those out. It could lead to further invitations from other readers' groups, writers' groups and even from librarians looking for speakers for the next World Book Day.

INDEPENDENT BOOKSHOPS

A rare breed these days but they do exist. If you know of one and have a print version of your book, I'd suggest an initial phone call to see if they'd be interested in taking some copies on sale or return. If they're willing, agree what their share of the cover price is going to be – most of the ones I've dealt with take a third – and how long they'll keep them for (they can't take up shelf space for too long if they're not selling). Then get something in writing formalizing your agreement. It's standard practice and doesn't imply a lack of trust. If a bookshop owner implies it does, walk away.

As your book is already on sale on the Internet, you may think this is a waste of time. It's not. You're competing against literally thousands of other titles so you want to make your book not just available but visible in as many places as possible.

Professional associations

If you haven't already done so, consider joining a professional association. The two main bodies in the UK are the Writers' Guild of Great Britain and the Society of Authors. Go to their respective websites and have a look at criteria for joining and then apply to whichever one suits your needs best.

The Society of Authors has very specific criteria for membership and, at the time of writing, will accept self-published writers only after they've achieved minimal sales of 300.

The Writers' Guild will accept you as a candidate member whether you've sold 300 copies, 30 or none just yet. At the time of writing you can join as a candidate for £100 a year. For that you get all the advantages of full membership – although no vote at the AGM – plus a weekly e-bulletin, *UK Writer* magazine to which you can submit articles and the chance to attend networking events.

My own experience of the Guild has been very positive and it was an article I wrote for *UK Writer* (edited by Tom) that led to this book being commissioned.

Income tax...

These are two words that can cause a lot of needless anxiety. I remember getting very stressed about keeping accounts and filling in a tax return when I first started earning money as a writer. This was because I'd listened to the people who'll tell you that all tax officers are heartless bloodsuckers. My actual experience was quite different and I found, as you will, that it's all pretty straightforward.

All you have to do is keep an accurate record of all your income as a writer and keep receipts for all those things you are able to claim for and set against tax. For example, you might be paid £100 for giving a presentation to a writers' group but have to pay £20 train fare to get there. So you'd deduct £20 from your fee and pay tax on £80. Just make sure you keep the train ticket as proof.

So keep both records and receipts and add them up every month.

If you go on the Internet and type 'tax advice for authors' into the search engine, you'll find general advice plus web pages for accountants who specialize in tax advice for writers. They will charge for their services, so weigh up your options. If your income at this stage is still low, you could contact the Citizens Advice Bureau for general free advice. You can also contact the tax office direct by phone or e-mail if you need further help.

The most important thing to remember is this: declare every penny you earn, only claim back what you're actually entitled to. If in doubt, ask.

Focus points

- You need a schedule that you are able to keep to.
- It must reflect a balance between your writing time, other commitments and your downtime.
- Try to make your writing times coincide as much as possible with the time of day you write best.
- Start extending your network via Twitter and Facebook.
- Start to build up a network of contacts in the local media.
- Seriously consider joining a professional association such as the Writers' Guild.
- Get into the habit of keeping accurate accounts.
- Declare every amount you earn as a writer.
- Never get creative with your claims for amounts to be set against tax.
- If in doubt, ask for help – you will get it!

Where to next?

In Chapter 12 we will consider how you can develop further.

12

The continuing need for self-development

Kevin McCann

Good writing, in my opinion, is – among other things – about self-development. It sets progressively higher standards, refuses to make do with second best and lowers your boredom threshold to almost zero.

Like all good relationships, it requires work and real commitment.

It's not always easy or even ultimately successful.

We write anyway because, in the end, we don't really want to do anything else.

And our best book will always be the one we write next.

Post-publication pitfalls

Once you've published your book, there are two major pitfalls you need to avoid – the smugs and the blues:

- **The smugs:** the belief that you can do no wrong, that everything you write will be brilliant and that all criticism of your new work springs from vile jealousy. When this wears off you may very well suffer...
- **The blues:** total depression characterized by excessive self-pity and melodrama. This can in turn lead to **writer's block:** the inability to write a single word down.

In my opinion, all three are different aspects of the same thing: fear of failure and/or fear of success.

What if... the book doesn't sell... it gets bad reviews or, worse yet, no reviews at all... Or it gets great reviews, it sells really well, everyone loves it, so the pressure's on. Or...

You could go on for ever, and being a writer – so probably a tad obsessive-compulsive – will be tempted to. You can analyse your feelings, talk things through, get in touch with your inner child... You could waste months of your life or you could recognize that depression almost always follows exhilaration and that the only way out of the maze is work.

So the first thing is: stick to your schedule. Yes, have a break from it all for a week or so. You've worked hard and achieved a lot so relax for a while. Just don't let a week turn into a month.

Secondly, when you do go back to your schedule, use your writing time for writing. I've found, for example, I can waste hours happily Facebooking, tweeting and generally losing myself in the Internet. It's marvellous in one way because you really can fool yourself into thinking that you're working. Of course, in a way, you are. You're marketing – but unless it's part of a thought-out pattern of activity, it will be about as much use as sharpening all your pencils and then colour-coding your socks.

Because you need to start writing again.

If a new book is already taking shape in your mind, then great. Get going. If not, don't despair. It's there but maybe needs a little coaxing.

So how do you write if you haven't got a single idea in your head?

Ways to start writing again

FREE-FALLING

This is also known as automatic writing. The method is very simple. You get either a notebook and pen or a screen and keyboard and then begin to write. Write the first thing that comes into your head and follow that with the second, then the third and so on. Don't plan what you're going to say in advance, well, not consciously anyway. Give yourself a time limit of ten minutes and stick to it.

At the end of the ten minutes read aloud what you've produced, but for the moment don't tinker with it. Just keep it safe.

THE FILM SCORE

Take any piece of instrumental music, play it and imagine it's part of the soundtrack of a film. Write the scene it goes with. I'd suggest you listen to it once, ponder for five minutes and then play it again while writing. In this case, your writing time will obviously be dictated by the length of the music.

LAST AND FIRST THOUGHTS

Keep a notebook by your bed. For about five or six minutes each night before you go to sleep, write down any thoughts that are going through your head. Repeat the exercise in the morning and then again that night and so on for about a week. Before you write each thought or thoughts *do not* go back and reread your last entry.

SERENDIPITY

Open a book, newspaper or magazine at random. Pick a sentence, close your eyes and then put your finger down on the text. Write down the words you've landed on and carry on from there. Again, give yourself a ten-minute time limit.

When you've finished these four exercises, read back through them all. Are there any common themes and/or images that occur in all four? If the answer's yes, as I suspect it will be, then that theme or image could be the starting point for your next book.

And while you're getting on with all that – or when you want a break from it – you might want to consider other ways of combining the need to raise your profile with your continuing development as a writer.

COMPETITIONS

Writing competitions generate very strong feelings in some people, though I really don't know why. At worst, you'll lose your entry fee and get very bitter when you read the winning entry. On the other hand, if you win or at least get placed, it will give your self-confidence a mighty boost and help get your name that bit more widely known.

There is often a set theme, a maximum word count and a closing date. Three factors guaranteed to focus your mind.

It's also worth remembering that, while not all competitions require an entry fee, most do, so never pay more than you can happily afford to lose.

E-ZINES

In Chapter 4 I mentioned freelance article writing, but just in case you haven't got round to that yet, I'll mention it again.

Victoria Roddam, publisher

'When it comes to non-fiction writing, and areas of "expertise" like knowledge of the publishing industry, or a psychology background, or a health expert background, it is useful for authors to raise their profile by contributing articles, or blogs, to specialist publications or online sites. Non-fiction publishers will often read or buy publications in the area in which they're looking to commission, and I would also say that online is probably the first port of call for many in this instance. Also, networking with others in the same field (so, comments on blogs, reviews, etc., as well as more traditional forms of networking) is useful because many publishers use recommendations, so the more people you know the better.'

What you need to be developing now is a portfolio – a selection of articles, reviews and so on which you've had published. Keep a record of where and when each was published – don't think you'll be able to remember, you won't – and as and when you come across magazines that you'd like to write for, contact the editor and ask if they'd be interested in seeing a sample of your work.

Keep a record of editors/magazines you've contacted and note the title of the sample piece you sent them. Also note the date you sent it and give them a realistic turn-around to get back to you.

When you find magazines that will take your work, stay with them and develop a good working relationship with your editor. Never miss a deadline, never be either over or under the word count, rewrite if you're asked to and always be polite.

Three last tips

1 Don't try to fake it. Write about topics that you've a genuine interest in and passion for. If you simply look at what's big right now, you could probably produce something that was informative and competent. If, on the other hand, you write about your passions, your work will have the potential to be so much more than that.

2 Be prepared to write for deferred payment, i.e. nothing in the short term. A small fee is always better than no fee at all, but in the long term a raised profile that could lead to you being talent-spotted is worth much more.

3 If you're unsure, ask for advice either publicly through online chat rooms or privately by contacting the Writers' Guild. In the end, though, trust your instincts.

Writers' retreats and residential courses

I've attended three of these and found them incredibly useful. Their main value was being away from the everyday world for five days and writing, sharing my work and worries with other writers and getting detailed feedback from a course tutor.

The only drawback is that they can be very pricey. However, if you live in the UK and want to attend one of the courses run by the Arvon Foundation (www.arvonfoundation.org), you might be eligible for a grant to help with the course fees. These grants are awarded on the basis of need and not your publishing record.

Find a writing course

Type 'writing courses' into your search engine followed by your location. List the ones that look the most useful and/or interesting. Give priority to your own type of writing – for example, if you're a novelist, attend novel writing courses – but include at least one that's dealing with a type of writing you've never tried before.

Then go to as many as you can. The day you think nobody can teach you anything is the day the writer in you expires. In fiction, brilliant people are almost always cutting, scornful and know everything. In reality, the best writers I've ever met have always been open-minded and curiously self-effacing.

Websites and blogs

Update both regularly and don't forget to put the link for your blog on the website and vice versa.

Raise your profile... but keep your credibility

Put the links for both your blog and website under your name whenever you send out an e-mail. People do look and it can lead to work.

In the 'About me' section of your website never lie, exaggerate or spin. If you do and get found out, your credibility will vanish.

And there's another reason too, although it's purely a personal opinion. I believe that when Shakespeare said, 'To thine own self be true', he wasn't just mouthing a platitude; he was sharing an insight.

Now we all know that your truth and mine may not coincide. Ask any police officer who's collected witness statements related to a traffic collision and they'll tell you that, if there are five witnesses, you'll get five different versions of the truth. What is important is that you, as a writer, remain faithful to your truth and tell it as best you can – so be honest in every aspect of your writing life.

Primary sources

As a child I was fascinated by my parents' and grandparents' tales of what I called the 'olden days'. I was given eyewitness accounts of among of the things, the 1914 Christmas Truce, the General Strike and the Blitz. And what had made these stories lodge in my mind was their human perspective.

At the age of 11, for example, I had only the vaguest understanding of the causes of the First World War but I did know that on Christmas Day, 1914, my granddad and his mates climbed out of their trenches and walked into no-man's-land.

His stories and those of my grandmother, mum and dad began as entertainments to while away wet afternoons in the days before daytime television. Their importance as my first encounters with story didn't become obvious until years later when I took part in a writing project based in Lancashire Archives.

I'd assumed before the project began that the archive itself would consist mainly of birth, marriage and death certificates and other official documents. I couldn't have been more wrong.

There were last wills dating back as far as the sixteenth century, postcards sent from France during the First World War, records of the local assizes, music – hall programmes, a thirteenth-century almanac, guest books from theatrical boarding houses ('Very many thanks, sincerely Harry Houdini') and the one that grabbed my attention – the patients' ledger, Lancaster Asylum, 1890.

I opened it at random. There was a full-page report: a name, an age, a description of the patient's condition on admission – 'imbecile' – a record of his stay and in the top left corner, his photograph. And, because he was looking straight at the camera, he now seemed to be looking at me. I turned the page to find a brief account of his sudden deterioration and death the following year.

I turned over to the next page. Above the name and condition – 'melancholia' – were two photographs. One of a smiling girl wearing a straw bonnet decorated with flowers. The other of an almost fleshless face framed by lank hair. It was mentioned in passing that she'd been force-fed daily.

Before this I'd seen archive material as nothing more than a research tool. The thought that it could act as a primary stimulus had never occurred to me. I started writing. Six poems about the patients in Lancaster Asylum came in as many days. I hadn't written so much in the last six months. And these were followed by another 30 on a wide variety of subjects. They weren't all prompted by the stories I'd heard as a child. Just the overwhelming majority of them.

The archive material had not just given me a starting point; it had reminded me of why I started writing in the first place. It wasn't for money or fame – though I wouldn't turn my nose up at either – it was because I felt passionately and wanted to express that passion through words. It had reawakened in me a point of view that apparent cynicism had all but totally obscured. And, of course, the apparent cynicism was just my cover story.

The simple truth was that I hadn't written anything for over six months. The result was that I had become very depressed and convinced that the rest really was going to be silence. Now, suddenly, the words were flowing and the poems more or less writing themselves.

I compared notes with other writers on the course and they all told the same story. Not only were they suddenly writing more, the quality of their work was, in many cases, better than it had ever been. This got me thinking.

Usually, when I need information I google in a few key words and see what comes up. If I want to know about conditions in nineteenth-century asylums, I can access, almost instantly, dozens of eyewitness accounts as well as extracts from official reports, annual death rates and so on. Or I can do what I actually did.

I can go to the main archives and look at the Record Book for the year 1890. I can feel the weight of it. If I press my face close enough to the pages, I can catch a smell, even if it's only imaginary, of carbolic. The same smell that would have filled the wards. I can look into the eyes of the inmates and imagine their lives all the more vividly.

I think I'd fallen into the error of thinking that, because I was now a published writer, I needed to concentrate my attentions not on those things I wanted to write, but on the things I felt I ought to write. I'd been deliberately suppressing anything that I thought wasn't worth my attention, which of course was everything in the end.

So, by all means, seek out gaps in the market, sit down and plan out a strategy – I do both – but write your passion, craft it, publish it, market it and hope it sells. No matter what else, write what you love to read.

And if, like me, you find yourself blocked, apart from the writing exercises to loosen you up, go to primary source material – old letters, diaries, news clippings... – and just start reading until something grabs your imagination. You'll know when it's happened because nothing else you try to read after that will go in.

Visit an archive

Type 'archon' into your search engine. This will lead you to the ARCHON Directory, which will give you the location of every archive in the UK, plus related archives in other parts of the world including the 275 to be found in the United States. Find your nearest archive and visit it.

Don't just go in and ask if you can have a browse. The material in archives, is stored and can only be initially accessed by archivists, so, when you go, have a specific area you want to look into. Phone or e-mail in advance and find out what the archive's system is. One very good way to start is to see if it has back copies of local newspapers. If so, pick a month and a year and start reading through. You'll find something. I guarantee it.

One picture is worth...

I've already mentioned the link between the written word and film (see Chapters 1 and 3) – how the fact that you can tell a good film from a bad one shows that you have a critical faculty which you must now develop and how a great deal of prose writing borrows from film to achieve its effects. Remember our bored teacher, Mary, leaning against the back classroom wall and feeling old?

I later went on to talk about the need to make your reader see whatever it is you're writing about and how all writing, whether it's fiction or non-fiction, contains a strong visual element.

Try this

Type 'scripts online' into your search engine. Two sites that are well worth a look are www.lazybeescripts.co.uk and www.simplyscripts.com.

Get into the habit of reading scripts regularly and, when you're reading them, as well as looking at the visual imagery start thinking about structure – that is, the way the film tells its story. Ask yourself questions such as:

- Is it a linear narrative that begins at the beginning and then goes through to the end in a straight line?
- Does it begin with a series of flashbacks?
- How does the script draw you in and then keep you interested?

Now obviously, not all cinematic techniques will translate into prose. Could you describe slow-motion in a story? Probably not, but could you slow-motion your prose in any way to create that effect? Remember: long sentences slow the pace of the story down; short ones speed it up.

If you're drawn to non-fiction, type 'online documentaries' into your search engine. You'll get a lot of hits and, again, as well as the choice of images, look at the way the story is told.

As well as film/documentary scripts, look at theatre scripts. On stage, unless it's some overblown musical, you're going to get a story that centres on dialogue and character. You can't hide behind special effects and cameos from big names. What you've got is an audience and an acting area.

The audience has paid and expect their interest to be held for anything up to three hours. So when you're reading stage scripts, look at the dialogue and how it's used to push along the story while simultaneously maintaining the illusion that what you're seeing are real conversations between real people.

Finally, go to www.bbc.co.uk/writersroom. As well as TV scripts, you'll also find radio scripts. Again, get into the habit of reading them regularly. Radio depends on sound, so, as well as voices, it uses sound effects. These combine with the listener's imagination and create the story. Read a couple of radio scripts and see how the writer makes it possible for the listener to keep track of who's talking at any one time. How is sound used to create atmosphere? Is there anything you can learn from that and apply to your own writing?

One last thought. Have you considered adding scriptwriting to your repertoire? Breaking into film or TV is very difficult but you might want to consider writing for the radio. The BBC Writersroom will read unsolicited scripts and their website regularly posts details of writing opportunities for aspiring scriptwriters.

Dealing with 'failure'

Let's suppose you've done everything right. Your book was edited, proofread, had a great cover, a snappy blurb and was well marketed but still isn't selling. What do you do?

- **Option 1:** Give up the whole idea and quietly withdraw.
- **Option 2:** Ask yourself why?

A good place to start is with your book itself. Reread it critically. You've now put enough distance between your manuscript and yourself to be able to do so objectively.

- What are its main strengths but, more importantly, what are its faults?
- Why did you write that particular book? Was it because you had to or because you felt you ought to?
- Why do you write at all?

HAD TO VS. OUGHT TO

A book or story, poem, script and so on should, ideally, be something you write because you feel compelled. The story won't leave you alone. It intrudes into your mind whether you want it there or not.

A book you feel you ought to write is one that you hope will impress people and make you famous. Nothing wrong with that, but has it got in the way of your own good judgement? Are you a novelist who really should be writing short stories? Or vice versa? Are you writing in the genre you're most passionate about? Maybe you've looked at what's selling, decided on, say, crime fiction, read a couple, drawn up a plan and then followed it. Slowly and laboriously and with no real joy at all.

Go back to basics here for a minute and ask yourself two simple questions.

1 Who are you?

2 What do you want?

Let's take the second question first. What I want is love, financial security and to write. And not just that, but to write well. Notice that I've mentioned money, because, in the real world, I need it to survive. And we all need love because, deep down inside, we're all just a bit insecure. But, above all, I want to write well. I want each thing I produce to be better than its predecessor. That's it.

Now, if I was answering the first question, my answer would be Kevin Patrick Michael McCann, aged well over 21, whose main passion in life is writing.

Which would lead me back to, *Why do you write?* And my answer to that would be because I have to.

Which prompts one last query: *How do you choose what to write?*

Well, the short answer is: I don't – it chooses me. However, I'm aware that sounds glib and evasive, so let me put it this way. When I'm writing something I want to write, I can't wait to get back to it. Anything else is a monumental effort that always sounds a false note.

Over the years I've tried out a lot of different types of writing apart from poetry – my main passion – and have made some interesting discoveries.

I started off wanting to be a serious poet (and, to some extent, I am) but for years I dismissed children's poetry as trivial, something only written by people who couldn't produce the 'real thing'. When I was finally challenged to produce some good children's poems, I discovered how wrong I was.

I found writing for children was a technical challenge I really enjoyed – they love rhyme but not jingles – and that editors liked my work. Now, I could go on and give you other examples but I don't have to because my point is simply this: for years I stubbornly refused to try my hand at particular kinds of writing because I wanted to be a serious writer and considered such trivialities as beneath me. It was only when I finally deigned to give it a go that I discovered:

- I was quite good at it and
- I really enjoyed it and, most important of all,
- my other work improved – considerably – because I'd reopened what was a closed mind.

So, if you haven't already considered it, how about now?

Writing for children

There's really only one good reason for writing for children: because you want to. If you think it's going be easy and very well paid and that you could end up doing a J.K. Rowling, you're probably going to bitterly disillusioned.

The simple truth, as I discovered, is that children are far more discriminating than most of us give them credit for. They know when they're being patronized, they hate being preached at – don't we all? – and they can be very perceptive.

If they don't like something, they'll tell you. If you ask them why they don't like something, they'll tell you. One other thing as well – they're usually right.

The same applies if they do like something.

So what do children like?

In my experience, they want a good story that is well told, has believable characters, even if it's a fantasy, and holds their attention. So the first thing you need to do is read lots of children's books. Go into bookshops and see what's both currently being published and selling.

Go into libraries and talk to a librarian. Find out what's being borrowed and what isn't, and then read the work that's popular and see what makes it popular. Do the same for the books that aren't going out and see if you can work out what's wrong.

When I was a teacher – I taught 11- to 18-year-olds – I discovered that a lot of the books aimed at the children's market were very worthy, contained strong moral messages and, for the most part, bored children rigid. I remember one class of adolescents who would literally throw their books at me if they weren't gripped within two pages. In sheer desperation, I tried them with *Call of the Wild* by Jack London. They loved it.

Now, on one level, it was simply because the central character was a dog. On a deeper level, it was because it was about a dog that was brutalized and in the end became savage before being finally rescued by a decent man. The message – brutality creates savagery – was one they clearly understood. The story rang true and the ending gave them consolation.

I think that's the key even when we're talking about fantasy. In the Harry Potter series Hogwarts is a dream school for apprentice wizards and witches who, just like any other school students, moan about their homework and dread exams. But it's also a place where people die, evil is real and it's OK to be scared. Just like the real world that children know exists because they see it on television every day.

Books about children's books

As well as reading books for children, read a few books *about* books for children. Apart from *Writing for Children* by Allan Frewin Jones and Lesley Pollinger, which is excellent by the way, have a look at J.R.R. Tolkien's essay 'On Fairy Stories'.

One last point. I mentioned earlier in the chapter how much I, as a child, enjoyed hearing about what I called the olden days. When I first started writing for children I used my own childhood as a starting point. I realized that, while the trappings of childhood change, the emotions don't. So I avoided specific contemporary references and concentrated on events and the emotions they generated.

When I was eight we had two TV channels, both black and white, and there were no such things as computer games. On the other hand, 'it' hurt just as much then as it does now – 'it' being anything from being ridiculed by a bully to the grief felt when someone you love dies. Children's emotions may be more magnified than those of adults – well, most thinking adults anyway – but they're just as real.

You might find it interesting to read *The Lore and Language of Schoolchildren* by Iona and Peter Opie. It was first published in 1959, so a lot of the material is out of date, but it's still one of the best insights into the way children think that I've ever read.

 Focus points

- Fear of failure, fear of success and writers' block are all aspects of the same thing.
- The only way forward is to keep raising your profile!
- Use archives not just as a source of research but also as a source of ideas.
- Continue reading.
- Look at different approaches to narrative, so read scripts as well as novels, short stories, biographies and so on.
- Ask yourself: Am I writing what I want to or what I feel I ought to?
- Consider writing for children, although you should bear in mind that it's not as easy as it looks. If you have the knack, however, it's incredibly rewarding.
- Keep writing!

Where to next?

In Chapter 13 we will consider how you can build and extend your writing career.

13

What next?

Kevin McCann

One thing I've learned is that, when it comes to writing, there's very little that can be just written hastily. Well, I suppose that's not quite true. Some things have almost written themselves and some would never have been written at all if it hadn't been for a magazine editor with a specific request. And when I was a student, I wrote thousands of words on subjects that didn't always set me on fire. I suspect it showed.

Everything I've ever written, whether it's been for money, love or both, has required effort and commitment. The more committed I am, the better – in theory – the writing becomes.

What I also discovered was that it was possible to write for money and produce work I was and still am proud of. I don't have an artistic hierarchy and I don't believe that my children's poems or articles for educational magazines get in the way of my adult poems and short stories.

Quite the opposite, in fact. It's all writing, and the different strands are no more separate than the threads that make up a spider's web are ultimately separate.

Writing to order (i.e. to a deadline with a specific word count) taught me the self-discipline I needed. It's the difference, I think, between being 'a writer' and writing.

Let me briefly explain.

In Liverpool we have a saying: 'If you can't fight, wear a big hat!' It's a saying I've often applied to the kind of people who read lots of books about writing, talk about the daily struggle with language, and their poor suffering souls, etc. I also found, oddly enough, that they all subscribed to the 'I can't get published because I didn't go to Oxbridge' conspiracy theories.

In my time, I've met dozens of them in the various writers' groups I've tutored. I discovered that their work rarely matched the build-up they gave it. I also discovered the person I call 'the quiet one at the back'. She or he would attempt all the writing exercises I set – but sometimes a bit quirkily – had done a lot of reading, rarely repeated a mistake and in the end, while agreeing with my criticism of their work, would often come up with a solution that was far better than mine. It was better than mine because it was a conclusion they'd arrived at by combining their own intelligence, their own experience and their own critical faculty.

It was always a moment I enjoyed because I knew they'd found their own voice and no longer needed either my approval or guidance. I'd also know that it wouldn't be much longer before we had the 'thanks for everything' conversation followed by the final parting of the ways. When that came, my last words to them were always: 'Will you carry on writing?'

That was an easy one and I always got a resounding yes.

The second and final question was always: 'And what's your ultimate ambition?'

You now have to answer the same two questions. I'm hoping that, having been through so much, the answer to the first question is yes. But what about the second question? What is your ultimate ambition?

Well, the answer I heard most frequently was: 'To be a full-time writer.'

If that's your ambition, good luck to you, but be realistic. You'll have to make money because you have to live. If you're making money, it's great. If you're not, it's sleepless nights, cheap but filling food and no social life. So, ideally, you're looking for the kind of writing that both pays and you're passionate about. Pash plus cash.

So, the next question is: can you make enough money to live on?

If not – well, at this stage anyway – can you combine a number of elements that together will give you enough of an income to get by? If you're lucky enough to have a full-time job, can you reduce your hours and give yourself more time to write?

If you're on your own, your decision affects nobody but you. If you share your life with somebody else, what are their thoughts? Because it's all very well being prepared to go without and sacrifice life's little luxuries, but it's not quite so good to expect other people to just blithely go along with you. Where I come from, that's called selfish. That's the polite version anyway. You could be lucky and your partner says – as mine did – 'Go for it!', but you need to have a plan:

- Make sure your income will still exceed your outgoings.
- Don't get a credit card and assume you'll be able to pay it off once the money starts rolling in. It might not.
- Try to build up a list of editors who both like your work and pay.
- Never assume that any magazine will last for ever.
- Look around for other sources of writing-related income.

Writers' workshops

If you've been a member of a writing class, then you'll know how they work and what people expect. So, could you run one? Now bear in mind that you're looking for income here as well as accolades, which means you'll have to charge.

So, do you know enough and, just as importantly, do you have enough natural authority to deal with the dynamics involved in keeping order? Do you have the patience to deal with the really difficult customer? Would you pay to be taught by you – if you see what I mean?

If the answer to any of the above is no, then you might want to seriously reconsider. For the moment, at least.

Unless you've already had some teaching experience, in which case all this will be blindingly obvious, I'd hold back and begin by getting some practical experience.

If you're a member of a group run by an accredited tutor who is being paid, then asking them whether they'd mind letting you practise chairing with a view to taking their job is probably not advisable. However, there's nothing to stop you observing their method and noticing how the session proceeds:

- Do they limit the time for each discussion on each piece of work?
- How do they deal with difficult students?
- Does the session include writing exercises?
- If so, when are they attempted? During the session or during the week?

If you're a member of a more informal group, ask if you can chair it. Do the same if it's a readers' group. In fact, if you're involved in any kind of group/organization that holds meetings, volunteer your services as chair.

And keep one very important fact in mind at all times: good teaching opens minds and bad teaching crushes potential. So it's not just a case of being confident enough to teach a group, it's also about having confidence in what you are teaching. It's no good having all the knowledge if you can't communicate that knowledge. It's no good having the gift of the gab if you've got nothing to say that's worth listening to. You need both.

 Remember this...

Good teaching like great acting looks effortless. It's not!

HOWEVER...

If you still want to try your hand at running a writers' group, you could set up some sampler sessions and see how things go. What you'll need initially is a free location (i.e. no fee for the use of the room) and a title that plays to your strengths. So, if you've published a novel, it's 'Writing a Novel: Getting Started'. If you write short stories, it's 'Writing Short Stories' and so on.

You already know how important a good eye-catching design is for a book cover, so apply the same knowledge to your poster. Ideally, what you want is something clear and concise. The title of the session, where it takes place, date and time (finish time as well as start time), your name and what you've published. I'd make it a one-off session to begin with and, initially, I'd make it free.

If things go well, you can look at setting up more sessions and maybe even charging a token fee to cover your expenses. At the time of writing, I know of a couple of groups that do just that. They meet weekly for two hours and each member pays £2 per session. The tutor obviously isn't making much money but isn't out of pocket either.

Scout a location

Find out if there are any writers' groups in either your local library or community centre. If there are, look further afield. The last thing you want is a feud with some already established group or groups. If you find a suitable location, approach the head librarian / centre manager and offer to run a free one-off sampler to gauge interest.

If this is agreed upon, have a look at the room you'll be using. Make sure that it's in a quiet location and that tables and chairs are available. Obvious, I know, but you'd be amazed how many times I've arrived somewhere and found four barstools and a coffee table next to the pinball machine.

Running a group

If you do get a group up and running, I would urge you to set out a few basic ground rules and stick to them:

- Comment on the work but not the individual.
- Don't insist on 'positive comments only' but do encourage the notion that negative comments should include a suggested improvement.

- The writer whose work is being discussed should only speak in response to a direct question but will get their chance to respond at the end.
- Speakers should never interrupt each other.

With regard to that last point, you must be able to direct the conversation. If everyone just jumps in as and when they feel like it, you'll end up with chaos. A number of years ago I was invited to a talking circle on a Native American reservation and saw the talking stick used very effectively to solve this problem. In that case it literally was a carved piece of wood. While someone was talking they held on to it, and when they'd finished they passed it to the next person in line.

It worked very well and I've used a similar device myself. Only in my case, it was a twelve-inch ruler. It did work, though!

Before we move on, here are a few helpful tips:

- Good teaching is like good cooking – it's all in the preparation – so go into each session with a writing idea just in case no one has brought any work to share. And have a backup... just in case they do the first piece of writing in ten minutes flat.
- Don't just recycle other people's ideas, come up with new ones of your own. But remember, if you do use someone else's idea, acknowledge them.
- Remember that people soon tire of gushing praise, so don't be afraid to be critical of a piece even if everyone else claims to love it. Your praise when it comes will carry more weight.
- Don't get involved in arguments about content. It's either well written or it's not. There are obvious exceptions to that suggestion. I once had a student read out a piece that was an incitement to race hate. So I talked about both content (vile) and style (crass).
- Make sure you set the agenda. Most students prefer it that way.
- Be consistent, don't play favourites, and hide any dislike you may feel towards individual students.
- By all means ask for feedback but don't keep asking for it. It may be a good idea to ask for something in writing at the end of your final session. It's often very useful.

One last thing. Not everyone can teach so, if it's not working out, walk away once you've fulfilled your commitments. But never walk out on a commitment unless you have absolutely no choice. You're only human, so nobody should expect you to be perfect, but they have a right to expect you to be reliable.

Here's a quotation for you to ponder:

Chas Parry-Jones, Ucheldre Arts Centre, Holyhead

'A good workshop leader needs to be a good and swift judge of character of his or her students, picking up their abilities and evaluating both their learning and listening capacity.'

Community arts

Find out what, if any, community arts projects are taking place in your area and try to get involved. You may not make any money but it will raise your profile, add to your experience, go on your CV and improve your chances of getting paid work further down the line.

If you haven't done it already, start subscribing to Arts Council England's jobs bulletin (www.artsjobs.org.uk). Apart from paid work, you'll see opportunities to get unpaid work experience. Now I subscribe to the notion of being paid for any work I do but I'm also prepared to work for no fee if it's for charity or if I'm likely to gain valuable experience.

Writer-in-residence

I've been a writer-in-residence several times. It's a position that can be useful for two main reasons:

1 It's usually paid *and*
2 It's often paid quite well.

That may sound cynical but, actually, it's not. It's realistic. The fees from a residency can buy you the peace of mind you need to get on with your own writing. The myth of the starving artist whose best work is forged in the white heat of poverty and noble thought is just that. What actually happens is that writers who are poor get on with their writing despite being poor, not because of it.

It's true that a good few years of going without can help you appreciate what life is really like for far too many people. George Orwell actually chose to live as a tramp and wrote up his experiences in *Down and Out in London and Paris*. He saw it as completing his education, but he also recognized that being poor is something to be endured but not desired.

Be warned, though. For every residency there will be dozens of applicants. They will all have track records in both publishing and community arts of one kind or another. So think of this as a long-term goal and start building up both your publishing record and your experience in running writers' groups.

If you manage to get the job, you'll find it very demanding. However, it will be valuable experience and, again, it adds to your credibility. One thing, though: read the terms and conditions very carefully. Make sure your hours and duties/responsibilities are clear. As a general rule, avoid anything that's open ended, for example '...and any other duties the line manager sees fit to designate'. All that really means is more work, same money. Ask any teacher.

If in doubt, get the contract looked at by an expert, so make sure you're in a professional association like the Writers' Guild before you sign. If whoever's managing the residency is insulted when you tell them you'd like a third party to look at the contract, assume they've got something to hide... so think hard before proceeding.

 ## Don't let yourself be exploited

If the contract is fine but later on in the residency you feel you're being exploited, go straight to your professional association and ask them for help and advice. You'll be doing yourself and every other writer a huge favour.

Approaching publishers

Have a look at the home pages of publishers that are interested in the kind of books you've either already written or want to write. Check what their submissions policy is. Some will want sample chapters plus a synopsis of a finished book but others will just want a proposal.

This, initially, would be a brief synopsis plus a short covering letter with some background information about yourself. Again, having a track record will help, but that, in itself, won't be enough. What you'll also need to do is convince a publisher to spend their money publishing your book.

So who is the book aimed at? The temptation here is to respond, 'People who can read!' – very witty, very unhelpful. So think carefully about this one. We'll come back to it in a minute.

What will make your book different? How will you make it stand out from its competitors? What you're looking for is a both a gap in the market and an original approach.

Do your market research

If you have an idea for a new and original book, do some market research before you start writing. Somebody else may have had the same idea and already written and published it.

Back in 1969, for example, George MacDonald Fraser published his first Flashman novel. He took the historical novel as his form and then proceeded to mix fact and fiction. The facts were his carefully researched accounts of actual events (First Afghan War, Indian Mutiny) as seen through the eyes of Harry Paget Flashman, the infamous bully who appears briefly in the almost unreadable *Tom Brown's Schooldays*.

His approach was to make Flashman a liar, cheat, racist, sexist lecher who fools everyone and ends up winning the Victoria Cross. The novels are Flashman's secret memoirs in which he tells nothing but the unvarnished truth.

The Flashman novels have three great strengths. They're meticulously researched. They're beautifully written and the first one was published in 1969. This was the year of Monty Python, Woodstock, the first Moon landing and riots in Derry. It was also a time when England's imperial past was no longer being seen as a source of pride.

Then along came Flashman, who was about as far removed from the 'play with a straight bat, stiff upper lip' myth of the British past as it was possible to get. Readers lapped it up. Of course, there are some who assume that because Flashman's a racist, the books are racist. They judge Huck Finn in the same way and simply can't see that the device being used here is irony.

Literary agents

If you've approached an agent or agents in the past, you'll already know all the dos and don'ts. But if you haven't...

Find an agent

Type 'literary agents' followed by your location (UK, USA, etc.) into your search engine. Go to each agency's home page, find their submissions policy and read it carefully.

If they clearly state that they don't look at unsolicited manuscripts, move on. Never write and ask whether they'd be willing to make an exception in your case. They won't. Not because they're being pedantic but because an agent can represent only a finite number of writers. There are, after all, only a finite number of hours in a week. It's as easy as that.

If they take unsolicited work, see if there's a reading fee. If there is, move on.

Of the agents left, find the ones who represent the kind of book that you've written. List them and then read their submissions guidelines – carefully! – and then stick to them.

The chances are they'll want a section of the manuscript (e.g. first three chapters) plus a brief summary of the plot. 'Brief' means about a thousand words or less. So you don't need to put in every tiny detail, just the main points.

Begin your brief summary with linked headings showing the flow of the narrative.

For example:

> Red Riding Hood sets off for G/ma's house – meets wolf in forest –
> wolf goes on ahead – eats G/ma – wolf disguises himself as
> G/ma – RRH arrives at cottage – wolf about to attack –
> huntsman bursts in & kills wolf – slices it open & out pops
> G/ma – all live happily ever, etc.

Now, as somebody who's told that story, I know that the above are
the barest of bare bones so in order to turn it into a synopsis, I'd
now need to flesh it out.

> Red Riding Hood sets out for Grandma's house – needs to
> deliver food as G/ma is sick – takes path through forest where
> she meets wolf, etc.

Again, as far as your covering letter goes, keep it brief and relevant.
You might want to start by giving a brief outline (about 200 words)
of your writing career to date (publications, your first book) but don't
waste words – limit yourself pretty much to that. When you're talking
about your book, you need to talk about its main theme (e.g. it's a
crime novel that explores a moral dilemma), your target readership
(teenagers, general readership, etc.) and point out why it's different
from every other book already published in the same genre.

Have a finished book

Only approach an agent if you have a finished book. If all
you've got is an idea/outline plus the first chapter and don't
want to write the rest on spec, go back to publishers who are
interested in proposals.

And remember, whether you've got a finished book or just an
outline, a good track record will help enormously.

If you're turned down, move on, but don't slam the door on your way
out. Reply to your rejection with a quick note thanking the agent for
their time. You never know when your paths might cross again.

Publisher seeks new writers...

Also be very aware that vanity publishers haven't gone away. They
dress themselves up as more plausible outfits these days but they're

still the same as they've always been. As a basic rule of thumb, anything that involves buying advance copies of your own book and claims about e-publishing being just a craze should be avoided.

The story so far

If this was a one-to-one surgery, I'd pause at this point, glance at my watch and then begin summing up. Before I do that, I've got one last thing I'd like you to do.

Assess your self-publishing skills

From memory, write out a list of all the skills you've acquired in the process of self-publishing your first book. I want you to do it from memory because I suspect that, as the list grows, it will have more impact than if you'd merely copied out the highlights of the chapter contents. Don't worry about getting them in chronological order. That's not the point of the exercise. What I want you to realize at this point is that with some help and advice from Tom and myself you've learned how to...

Now make that list.

When you've finished that, make a list of everything you've published or had published to date. Again, do this from memory.

Finally, look back through the contents section of this book and see how your memory compares with the full list of all the things you've actually learned.

Compare your list of remembered publications with the actual list on your CV.

Now, let's analyse the results and ponder their implications.

SKILLS

That should be a pretty long and impressive list by now. If, as I suspect, your memory fell short of your actual achievements, then so much the better. It only further reinforces my point that you probably know considerably more than you give yourself credit for. Now pause for a minute and think about that.

Whether you found the whole process comparatively easy – in which case you have natural ability – or quite hard work – in which case you're not one of those people who want it all on a plate – the fact is, you've written, edited, proofread and published a book.

That's a hell of an achievement so be proud of yourself – just don't get arrogant!

Publications

If your list of publications consists of nothing but your first book, then you do need to start doing something about that. Or, rather, if you want to move into the world of professional writing, you'll *really* need to start doing something about that. It very much depends on what you want and you simply may not want to go through all that again. Well, not yet anyway.

Or you may have a full-time job that you love and are perfectly content to self-publish every few years for a comparatively small readership.

The most important thing of all is this: write your passion and don't just hope for the best – strive for it.

If your first book was fiction but you've developed an interest in a non-fiction subject and want to write about that next, then go for it. It's not that art is better than academe or vice versa. They're both equally important. The academic explains how the world works. The artist interprets it. Value them both.

And finally...

Always remember that books like this one are helpful in showing how to take your knowledge and experiences and apply them to a practical end. In this case, writing and self-publishing. They will often confirm what you've suspected all along. They help you avoid mistakes and guide you to a successful conclusion, but they can never be a substitute for knowledge and experience.

You need to acquire that for yourself.

Now take everything that you know and keep writing.

And good luck.

Resources and further reading

Ebooks

Publish on Amazon Kindle with Kindle Direct Publishing
(free e-book)

*Smashwords Book Marketing Guide: How to Market Any Book
for Free* (free e-book)

How to Self-Publish: A Guardian Masterclass
(Guardian Shorts, e-book)

Websites

Self-publishing showcase:
www.theguardian.com/books/series/self-publishing-showcase

Design: www.thebookdesigner.com

Guidance on writing, publishing and self-publishing:
http://authonomy.com/writing-tips

Publishing and self-publishing news: www.publishersweekly.com

Marketing discussions and ideas: http://sethgodin.typepad.com

Reading

The list that follows is not meant to be seen in any way as an
ignore-the-rest-because-this-is-best: it's entirely personal. As we have
already stated, if you write you should read, and read widely. So, as
well as making use of libraries and bookshops, scour the shelves of
charity shops. Follow your own passions, but maybe try some of the
following as well:

Dictionary of Literary Terms and Literary Theory (published by
Penguin)

One of the most useful and illuminating books I've ever come across.

Writing a Novel by John Braine

Becoming a Writer by Dorothea Brande

On Writing by Stephen King

The Art of Fiction by David Lodge

Four excellent books – all very readable and all very useful. However, don't take my word for it. Read them and then make up your own mind.

Nights at the Circus by Angela Carter
Excellent introduction to magic realism – if you don't know what that term means, look it up – and a page-turner to boot.

Heart of Darkness by Joseph Conrad
This is worth reading for the descriptive passages alone. Try reading them aloud.

Great Expectations by Charles Dickens
I think this is Dickens' most subversive book – which is probably why I like it.

The Great Gatsby by F. Scott Fitzgerald
Beautifully written – again, try reading it aloud. On the surface it's about a doomed passion but there's much more than that going on.

I, Claudius by Robert Graves
Excellent example of first-person narrative and a page turner to boot.

Catch 22 by Joseph Heller
Any book whose title becomes part of the language has to be worth looking at. Although it's set in World War II, it has an oddly contemporary feel.

The Perfect Spy by John Le Carré and *Mother Night* by Kurt Vonnegut
Try reading these back to back. On the surface they're both very different books but in terms of theme... well read them and, again, decide for yourself.

The Call of the Wild by Jack London
Simply excellent. If you enjoy it, try *White Fang* and then round off with *Tarka the Otter* by Henry Williamson

Doctor Zhivago by Boris Pasternak
Everyone who's either seen the David Lean film or the TV version thinks they know what this book's about. They don't. Read it for yourself and find out why.

Wuthering Heights by Emily Brontë
Her only novel, this owes a great deal (like so many others) to both folk and fairy tales.

On Fairy Stories by J.R.R. Tolkien
This is a very readable discussion of fantasy/fairy tales that analyses both how and why they appeal. It contains the best reply to people who dismiss escapist stories I've ever read.

Danse Macabre by Stephen King
There's an extensive watch this / read this list at the back which is well worth a look... even if fantasy isn't your genre. For example, find out what King means by the phrase 'phobic pressure points' and then see whether it might apply to your own work.

The Haunting of Hill House by Shirley Jackson
One of the best, if not the very best, haunted house novel ever written. There's an interesting story about how Shirley Jackson got the idea in the first place which you may find useful.

The ghost stories of M.R. James
These stories are masterpieces of subtlety and suggestion that set a standard for everything that followed.

The Book of Fantasy, edited by Jorge Luis Borges, Silvina Ocampo and Adolfo Bioy Casares
Unlike most genre anthologies, this isn't simply a rehash of all the others and includes some genuine rarities.

The Fall and Rise of Reggie Perrin by David Nobbs
This is a classic – to 'do a Reggie Perrin' has now entered the language – just read it.

The Hard Life by Flann O'Brien
This includes a character who runs correspondence courses in Tightrope Walking – which should give you a clue. If you enjoy this, try *The Third Policeman*.

Decline of the English Murder by George Orwell.
This begins with a short essay on murder (and our fascination with it) that's as relevant today as when it was first written. It also contains essays on Dickens and Kipling that make for excellent introductions to their work. Also, try tracking down Raymond Chandler's essay 'The Simple Art of Murder' and, again, read the two back to back.

The Big Sleep by Raymond Chandler
Phillip Marlowe is the archetype of all private eyes and you'll either be confused or hooked by Chapter 5. It's beautifully written, although Chandler has been criticized for being too poetic... which is like criticizing strawberries for being just too delicious.

The Night of the Hunter by Davis Grubb
Most of you will know this through the film version starring Robert Mitchum. The book is well worth tracking down. Again, it's wonderfully well written and is in a direct line of descent from every big bad wolf story ever told.

Red Harvest by Dashiell Hammet
Hammet had actually been a private investigator, so his stories have that extra whiff of seedy authenticity. Unlike Chandler, his prose style was very simple. He proves that really great writing is not about using extraordinary language; it's about using ordinary language to do extraordinary things.

Voice of the Fire by Alan Moore
Short stories all set in and around Northampton – beginning about 4000 BC and ending in the twentieth century.

Metamorphosis by Franz Kafka
Kafka's name alone scares off a lot of people – they imagine something so highbrow as to be almost unreadable – they're wrong. Try this story as an introduction to his work. It's a direct descendant of many a folk tale and is the ancestor of horror films like *The Fly*.

Index